# Cliffs

**D0686140**

# The Crucible

### By Jennifer L. Scheidt

## IN THIS BOOK

- Find out about Arthur Miller and his writing
- Preview an Introduction to the Play
- Explore themes, character development, and recurring images in the Critical Commentaries
- Savor in-depth character analyses
- Understand the play better through the Critical Essays
- Reinforce what you learn with CliffsNotes Review
- Find additional information to further your study in CliffsNotes Resource Center and online at www.cliffsnotes.com

## Hungry Minds™

Best-Selling Books • Digital Downloads • e-Books • Answer Networks • e-Newsletters • Branded Web Sites • e-Learning
New York, NY • Cleveland, OH • Indianapolis, IN

**About the Author**
Jennifer L. Scheidt received her M.A. from the University of Texas at San Antonio and now is a full-time instructor at Palo Alto Community College in San Antonio, Texas, where she teaches various writing and literature courses.

**Publisher's Acknowledgments**
**Editorial**
Project Editor: Kathleen M. Cox
Acquisitions Editor: Greg Tubach
Copy Editor: Corey Dalton
Glossary Editors: The editors and staff of Webster's New World Dictionary
Editorial Assistant: Carol Strickland

**Production**
Indexer: York Production Services, Inc.
Proofreader: York Production Services, Inc.
Hungry Minds Indianapolis Production Services

**CliffsNotes *The Crucible***

Published by:
**Hungry Minds, Inc.**
909 Third Avenue
New York, NY 10022
www.hungryminds.com
www.cliffsnotes.com (CliffsNotes Web site)

ISBN: 0-7645-8588-6

Printed in the United States of America

10 9 8 7 6 5 4 3

1V/QW/RR/QR/IN

Distributed in the United States by Hungry Minds, Inc.

Library of Congress Cataloging-in-Publication Data
Scheidt, Jennifer L., 1971–
    CliffsNotes The Crucible / Jennifer L. Scheidt.
        p. cm.
    Includes bibliographical references and index.
    ISBN 0-7645-8588-6 (alk. paper)
    1. Miller, Arthur, 1915– Crucible--Examinations--Study guides.2. Historical drama, American--Examinations--Study guides. 3. Salem (Mass.) in literature. 4 Witchcraft in literature I. Title: Miller's The Crucible. II. Title.
PS3525.I5156.C737 2000
812'.52--dc21                                        00–035108
                                                                CIP

Distributed by CDG Books Canada Inc. for Canada; by Transworld Publishers Limited in the United Kingdom; by IDG Norge Books for Norway; by IDG Sweden Books for Sweden; by IDG Books Australia Publishing Corporation Pty. Ltd. for Australia and New Zealand; by TransQuest Publishers Pte Ltd. for Singapore, Malaysia, Thailand, Indonesia, and Hong Kong; by Gotop Information Inc. for Taiwan; by ICG Muse, Inc. for Japan; by Norma Comunicaciones S.A. for Columbia; by Intersoft for South Africa; by Eyrolles for France; by International Thomson Publishing for Germany, Austria and Switzerland; by Distribuidora Cuspide for Argentina; by LR International for Brazil; by Galileo Libros for Chile; by Ediciones ZETA S.C.R. Ltda. for Peru; by WS Computer Publishing Corporation, Inc., for the Philippines; by Contemporanea de Ediciones for Venezuela; by Express Computer Distributors for the Caribbean and West Indies; by Micronesia Media Distributor, Inc. for Micronesia; by Grupo Editorial Norma S.A. for Guatemala; by Chips Computadoras S.A. de C.V. for Mexico; by Editorial Norma de Panama S.A. for Panama; by American Bookshops for Finland. Authorized Sales Agent: Anthony Rudkin Associates for the Middle East and North Africa.

For general information on Hungry Minds' products and services please contact our Customer Care department; within the U.S. at 800-762-2974, outside the U.S. at 317-572-3993 or fax 317-572-4002.

For sales inquiries and resellers information, including discounts, premium and bulk quantity sales and foreign language translations please contact our Customer Care department at 800-434-3422, fax 317-572-4002 or write to Hungry Minds, Inc., Attn: Customer Care department, 10475 Crosspoint Boulevard, Indianapolis, IN 46256.

For information on licensing foreign or domestic rights, please contact our Sub-Rights Customer Care department at 212-884-5000.

For information on using Hungry Minds' products and services in the classroom or for ordering examination copies, please contact our Educational Sales department at 800-434-2086 or fax 317-572-4005.

Please contact our Public Relations department at 212-884-5163 for press review copies or 212-884-5000 for author interviews and other publicity information or fax 212-884-5400.

For authorization to photocopy items for corporate, personal, or educational use, please contact Copyright Clearance Center, 222 Rosewood Drive, Danvers, MA 01923, or fax 978-750-4470.

**Hungry Minds**™ is a trademark of Hungry Minds, Inc.

# Table of Contents

# How to Use This Book

CliffsNotes *The Crucible* supplements the original work, giving you background information about the author, an introduction to the play, a graphical character map, critical commentaries, expanded glossaries, and a comprehensive index. CliffsNotes Review tests your comprehension of the original text and reinforces learning with questions and answers, practice projects, and more. For further information on Arthur Miller and *The Crucible,* check out the CliffsNotes Resource Center.

CliffsNotes provides the following icons to highlight essential elements of particular interest:

Reveals the underlying themes in the work.

Helps you to more easily relate to or discover the depth of a character.

Uncovers elements such as setting, atmosphere, mystery, passion, violence, irony, symbolism, tragedy, foreshadowing, and satire.

Enables you to appreciate the nuances of words and phrases.

## Don't Miss Our Web Site

Discover classic literature as well as modern-day treasures by visiting the Cliffs-Notes Web site at www.cliffsnotes.com. You can obtain a quick download of a CliffsNotes title, purchase a title in print form, browse our catalog, or view online samples.

You'll also find interactive tools that are fun and informative, links to interesting Web sites, tips, articles, and additional resources to help you, not only for literature, but for test prep, finance, careers, computers, and Internet too. See you at www.cliffsnotes.com!

# LIFE AND BACKGROUND OF THE PLAYWRIGHT

# Personal Background

Arthur Miller was born in Harlem on October 17, 1915, the son of Polish immigrants, Isidore and Augusta Miller. Miller's father had established a successful clothing store upon coming to America, so the family enjoyed wealth; however, this prosperity ended with the Wall Street Crash of 1929. Financial hardship compelled the Miller family to move to Brooklyn in 1929.

## Education

Miller graduated from high school in New York in 1933. He applied to Cornell University and the University of Michigan, but both schools refused him admission. Miller worked a variety of odd jobs—including hosting a radio program—before the University of Michigan accepted him. At school, he studied journalism, became the night editor of the *Michigan Daily,* and began experimenting with theater.

## Jobs

In addition to hosting a radio program, Miller held a variety of jobs during his early career. After he left the University of Michigan, Miller wrote plays for the Federal Theatre in 1939. The Federal Theatre provided work for unemployed writers, actors, directors, and designers. Congress closed the Federal Theatre late in 1939.

# Career Highlights

Miller's prolific writing career spans a period of over sixty years. During this time, Miller has written twenty-six plays, a novel entitled *Focus* (1945), several travel journals, a collection of short stories entitled *I Don't Need You Anymore* (1967), and an autobiography entitled *Timebends: A Life* (1987). Miller's plays generally address social issues and center around an individual in a social dilemma, or an individual at the mercy of society.

Miller's first play, *No Villain,* produced in 1936, explores Marxist theory and inner conflict through an individual facing ruin as a result of a strike. *Honors at Dawn,* 1937, also centers around a strike and contrasting views of the economy, but focuses on an individual's inability to express himself. *The Great Disobedience,* 1938, makes a connection between the prison system and capitalism. *The Golden Years,* 1940, tells the story of Cortes despoiling Mexico, as well as the effects of capital-ism and fate on the individual.

Miller produced two radio plays in 1941: *The Pussycat and the Expert Plumber Who Was a Man,* and *William Ireland's Confession.* Miller's third radio play, *The Four Freedoms,* was produced in 1942.

*The Man Who Had All the Luck,* 1944, revolves around a person who believes he has no control over his life, but is instead the victim of chance. *All My Sons,* 1947, explores the effect of past decisions on the present and future of the individual. *Death of a Salesman,* 1949, addresses the loss of identity, as well as a man's inability to accept change within himself and society. *The Crucible,* 1953, recreates the Salem witch trials, focusing on paranoid hysteria as well as the individual's struggle to remain true to ideals and convictions.

*A View from the Bridge,* 1955, details three people and their experi-ences in crime. *After the Fall,* 1964, focuses on betrayal as a trait of humanity. *Incident at Vichy,* 1964, confronts a person's struggle with guilt and responsibility. *The Price,* 1968, tells the story of an individual confronted with free will and the burden of responsibility.

*Fame,* 1970, tells the story of a famous playwright who is confronted but not recognized. *The American Clock,* 1980, focuses on the Depres-sion and its effects on the individual, while *Elegy for a Lady,* 1982, addresses death and its effects on relationships. *Some Kind of Love Story,* 1982, centers on society and the corruption of justice.

*The Ride Down Mountain Morgan,* 1991, centers around a man who believes he can obtain everything he wants. *The Last Yankee,* 1993, explores the changing needs of individuals and the resulting tension that arises within a marriage. *Broken Glass,* 1994, tells the story of indi-viduals using denial as a tool to escape pain.

Miller wrote the screenplay for the movie version of *The Crucible,* which was produced in 1996.

Miller has received numerous honors and awards throughout his career. Miller's accolades include: the Michigan's Avery Hopwood Award, 1936 and 1937; the Theatre Guild's Bureau of New Plays Award, 1937; the New York Drama Critic's Circle Award, 1947; the Pulitzer Prize, 1949; the New York Drama Critic's Circle Award, 1949; the Antoinette Perry and Donaldson Awards, 1953; and the Gold Medal for Drama by the National Institutes of Arts and Letters, 1959. Miller was also elected President of PEN (Poets, Essayists, and Novelists) in 1965.

# INTRODUCTION TO THE PLAY

# Introduction

Inspired by the McCarthy hearings of the 1950s, Arthur Miller's play, *The Crucible,* focuses on the inconsistencies of the Salem witch trials and the extreme behavior that can result from dark desires and hidden agendas.

Miller bases the play on the historical account of the Salem witch trials. In particular he focuses on the discovery of several young girls and a slave playing in the woods, conjuring—or attempting to conjure—spirits from the dead. Rather than suffer severe and inevitable punishment for their actions, the girls accused other inhabitants of Salem of practicing witchcraft. Ironically, the girls avoided punishment by accusing others of the very things of which they were guilty. This desperate and perhaps childish finger-pointing resulted in mass paranoia and an atmosphere of fear in which everyone was a potential witch. As the number of arrests increased, so did the distrust within the Salem community. A self-perpetuating cycle of distrust, accusation, arrest, and conviction emerged. By the end of 1692, the Salem court had convicted and executed nineteen men and women.

Miller creates an atmosphere and mood within the play reminiscent of the historical period and of Puritan culture. The inhabitants of Salem lived in a restrictive society. Although the Puritans left England to avoid religious persecution, they based their newly established society upon religious intolerance. The Puritans demonstrated their faithfulness, honesty, and integrity through physical labor and strict adherence to religious doctrine. They considered material and physical wants—especially sexual desires—as the Devil's work and a threat to society. The Bible and the minister's interpretation of the Bible determined what was considered socially acceptable behavior. The Puritans had no tolerance for inappropriate or unacceptable behavior and punished individuals publicly and severely if they transgressed. Miller captures the intolerance and religious fanaticism of the period and effectively incorporates them into the play.

Reading about the Salem witch trials and the paranoid frenzy going on at the time is one thing, but witnessing the trials first hand is quite another experience. Miller permits the audience to do just that by transforming the faceless names from history into living, breathing characters with desires, emotions, and freewill. Miller did make adjustments to the ages, backgrounds, and occupations of several of the individuals mentioned in the historical records, however. For example, he lowers the age gap between John Proctor and Abigail Williams from sixty and eleven, respectively, to thirty-five and seventeen, enabling the plot line of an affair between the two. Proctor and his wife Elizabeth ran an inn as well as a farm, but Miller eliminates this detail. Proctor's friend Giles Corey was actually pressed to death a month after Proctor's execution; however, Miller juxtaposes his death and Proctor's. Finally, Miller chose to omit the fact that Proctor had a son who was also tortured during the witch trials because he refused to confess to witchcraft.

Although no one can know for certain what the actual individuals thought, felt, or believed, Miller's incorporation of motive into the play's characters provides his audience with a realistic scenario that is both believable and applicable to society. For example, when the play was first produced during the 1950's, as McCarthyism submerged America in paranoia and fear, audiences could relate to the plot because Americans were turning in their friends so they would not be labeled as Communists. Although today's society may not be engaged in so-called "witch hunts," stories of an individual attempting to reestablish a relationship with a former lover by eliminating what he or she perceives to be the only obstacle—the person currently involved in a relationship with the former lover—are not uncommon. This classic love triangle appears repeatedly in literature, not to mention the supermarket tabloids.

Miller's exploration of the human psyche and behavior makes the play an enduring masterpiece, even though McCarthyism has faded into history. On one hand Miller addresses a particularly dark period in American history—a time in which society believed the Devil walked the streets of Salem and could become manifest in anyone, even a close neighbor or, worse yet, a family member. On the other hand, Miller moves beyond a discussion of witchcraft and what really happened in Salem to explore human motivation and subsequent behavior. The play continues to affect audiences by allowing them to see how dark desires and hidden agendas can be played out.

Abigail is a young woman who seizes an opportunity to reverse fate. She has had an affair with Proctor, who now refuses to continue the affair out of a mixture of guilt and loyalty to his wife. Abigail takes advantage of the chance to eliminate Proctor's wife by accusing her of witchcraft, giving Abigail the opportunity to marry Proctor, while elevating herself within the Salem community. Although Abigail enjoys being the chief witness of the court, her chief desire is to obtain Proctor, and she will do anything to bring this about, including self-mutilation and murder.

The Putnams also seize opportunity. The Royal Charter was revoked in 1692 and original land titles became invalid, creating a crisis of property rights. Individuals no longer felt secure with their landholdings because they could be reassigned at any time. As a result, neighbors distrusted one another and feuds broke out regarding property rights and clear deeds of ownership. Miller incorporates this aspect of the period into the play through the character of Mr. Putnam. Like Abigail, a hidden agenda guides Putnam, namely his greed for land. He, too, will stop at nothing to satisfy his desire, even if attaining his goal means murdering his neighbors by falsely accusing them of witchcraft so he can purchase their lands after their executions.

Miller's title, *The Crucible,* is appropriate for the play. A crucible is a container made of a substance that can resist great heat; a crucible is also defined as a severe test. Within the context of the play the term takes on a new meaning: not only is the crucible a test, but a test designed to bring about change or reveal an individual's true character. The witch trials serve as a metaphorical crucible, which burns away the characters' outer shells to reveal their true intentions and character beneath. Throughout the play, Miller carefully peels away the layers of each character so that the audience not only can identify the character's motivation, but also can reevaluate the character through his or her actions. In other words, the audience observes the character as he or she is tested, and the audience ultimately determines if he or she passes the test.

Proctor provides an excellent example. His affair with Abigail results in a fall from grace, not only with his wife Elizabeth, but also within himself. Proctor believes he is damned and cannot possibly regain Elizabeth's love and respect, not to mention his own self-respect and moral uprightness. Proctor is tested severely when he goes to the court to defend Elizabeth. In order to save his wife, he must publicly announce his sin and, therefore, lose his good name. Although he gives up his good name in court, he regains it at the end of the play by destroying his signed confession. The audience watches Proctor as the play progresses and judges his actions according to his motivations and reactions to the various "tests" through which he passes. As the audience observes the characters, the audience itself is tested and forced to acknowledge that desire—whether positive, such as the desire for pleasure, or negative, such as lust, greed, or envy—is a realistic part of life. The realization that desire affects individuals and their behavior keeps the audience engrossed in the play. *The Crucible* is divided into four acts; however, Miller does not include scene breaks within the play. It is possible to break each act into several scenes based upon shifts in location, and the entry and/or exit of characters.

The original version of the play included an encounter between John Proctor and Abigail in the woods; however, Miller chose to remove Act II, Scene 2, as it changed the dynamics of the play. This scene is generally included in the appendix of publications, but is rarely included in production of the play.

## A Brief Synopsis

*The Crucible* takes place in Salem, Massachusetts, in 1692. The action begins in the home of Reverend Parris, whose daughter Betty lies unconscious and appears very ill. Around midnight the night before, Parris had discovered Betty, his niece Abigail, and Tituba, his black slave, dancing in the woods, causing Betty to swoon. The local physician is unable to determine the cause of Betty's illness. Mr. and Mrs. Putnam arrive and reveal that their daughter Ruth is also ill. There is talk in the village of an unnatural cause.

Abigail warns her friend Mercy Lewis and the Proctors' servant Mary Warren not to reveal that they were all casting spells in the woods. Betty wakes, and Abigail threatens the other girls with violence if they tell anyone that she drank blood and cast a spell in order to kill Goody Proctor. Betty loses consciousness again.

John Proctor and Abigail talk privately about their former relationship. Prior to the opening of the play, Abigail worked as a servant in the Proctor home. Elizabeth Proctor was ill at the time and Abigail took on more responsibility within the Proctor household. When Elizabeth discovered the affair, she dismissed Abigail. During their discussion, Abigail becomes angry with Proctor because he refuses to acknowledge any feelings for her.

Betty wakes again and is hysterical. The well-respected Rebecca Nurse is visiting the Parris household and calms her. Prophetically, Rebecca warns Parris that identifying witchcraft as the cause of Betty's illness will set a dangerous precedent and lead to further problems in Salem. Mr. Putnam asks Rebecca to visit Ruth and attempt to wake her. Ruth is the only Putnam child to survive infancy, and Mrs. Putnam is jealous of Rebecca because all of Rebecca's children are healthy, whereas Mrs. Putnam had lost seven infant children.

Putnam, Proctor, and Giles Corey argue with Parris about his salary and other expectations. Parris claims that a faction is working to drive him out of town, and he disputes their salary figures. Putnam, Proctor, and Corey then begin arguing over property lines and ownership. Putnam accuses Proctor of stealing wood from land that he does not own, but Proctor defends himself, stating that he purchased the land from Francis Nurse five months ago. Putnam claims Francis had no right to the land and, therefore, could not sell it.

Reverend Hale arrives from another town to investigate the strange events in Salem. The people of Salem have summoned him as an expert in witchcraft to determine if witchcraft is behind the children's illnesses. Hale learns that the girls were dancing in the woods with Tituba, and that Tituba can conjure spirits. Abigail blames Tituba for enticing her to sin. Hale then questions Tituba, and she admits that she has seen the Devil, as has Goody Good and Goody Osburn. Abigail also confesses to witchcraft, stating that she had given herself to the Devil, but that she now repents. Betty wakes up, and she and Abigail name individuals that they say they have seen with the Devil.

Eight days later, Elizabeth discovers that Proctor spoke to Abigail privately while in Salem. Elizabeth and Proctor argue over this. Mary Warren comes home from Salem where she is serving as an official of the court, and gives Elizabeth a poppet (doll) that she made for her while sitting in the courtroom. Mary Warren tells Proctor that some of the girls accused Elizabeth of witchcraft, but the court dismissed the charge because Mary Warren defended her.

Hale arrives at the Proctor house and questions Proctor about his poor church attendance. He asks Proctor to name the Ten Commandments. Proctor names nine successfully, but he forgets the commandment forbidding adultery. Hale questions Elizabeth as well. Proctor reveals that Abigail admitted to him that the witchcraft charges were false.

Marshal Herrick then arrives and arrests Elizabeth. Earlier that evening, Abigail feels a needle-stab while eating dinner, and she accuses Elizabeth of attempted murder. The authorities of Salem search the Proctor house and discover the poppet, along with a needle. Hale questions Mary Warren and learns that she sewed the poppet and stored the needle inside. Mary Warren also tells him that Abigail saw her sew the poppet and store the needle. Nevertheless, Elizabeth is arrested.

The court convicts Martha Corey and Rebecca Nurse of witchcraft. Giles Corey tells the court he has proof that Putnam is accusing his neighbors of witchcraft in order to gain their land. Judge Danforth asks the name of the witness who gave Corey the information, but Corey refuses to cooperate. The court arrests him. Judge Danforth informs Proctor that Elizabeth is pregnant.

Mary Warren tells the court that she pretended to see spirits and falsely accused others of witchcraft. She reveals that Abigail and the other girls are also lying. Abigail denies Mary Warren's charge, however, and she and the others claim that Mary Warren is sending out her spirit against them in the court.

Proctor denounces Abigail's charge against Mary Warren, stating that Abigail is a lying whore. Proctor informs the court of his affair with Abigail and states that she is lying in order to have Elizabeth executed, thereby providing herself with the opportunity to become his wife. After Proctor agrees that Elizabeth would never lie, the court summons Elizabeth and questions her about the affair. Not knowing that her husband has confessed it, Elizabeth lies about the affair and is returned to jail. Abigail resumes her claim that Mary Warren is attacking her until Mary Warren recants her confession that she lied about the witchcraft and charges John Proctor as the Devil's man.

Several months pass. Proctor is in prison, scheduled to hang, along with Rebecca Nurse. Elizabeth is also in prison, although the court has delayed her execution until after she gives birth. Hale attempts to convince the prisoners to confess rather than hang, but all refuse. Proctor confesses and signs a written affidavit, but he destroys the document rather than have it posted on the church door. Proctor is taken to the gallows.

## List of Characters

**Reverend Parris** Minister in Salem. He believes a faction plans to force him to leave Salem, so he attempts to strengthen his authority through the witch trial proceedings.

**Betty Parris** Parris' daughter. Her father discovers her dancing in the woods, and she later accuses individuals of practicing witchcraft.

**Abigail Williams** Parris' niece. She instigates the witch trials by falsely accusing others of witchcraft. She pretends to see spirits and instructs the other girls to pretend as well.

**Tituba** Parris' black slave. Parris discovers her casting spells and making potions with the girls in the woods.

**Mrs. Ann Putnam** Wife of Thomas Putnam. She believes that a witch is responsible for the deaths of her seven infant children. Her jealousy of Rebecca Nurse leads her to accuse Goody Nurse of being a witch.

**Thomas Putnam** A greedy landowner in Salem. He systematically accuses his neighbors of witchcraft so that he might purchase their lands after they hang.

**Ruth Putnam** The Putnams' daughter. She accuses individuals of practicing witchcraft. A witness claims to have heard Putnam say Ruth's accusations helped him obtain land.

**Mary Warren** Servant to the Proctors. She goes along with Abigail and the girls by falsely accusing others of witchcraft; however, she later admits that she was lying.

**Mercy Lewis** Servant to the Putnams and friend to Abigail. She participates in the witch trials by pretending to see spirits and falsely accusing individuals of witchcraft.

**John Proctor** Salem farmer and former lover of Abigail's. He openly denounces Parris and does not attend church.

**Elizabeth Proctor** Wife of John Proctor. She is a decent and honest woman, who dismissed Abigail because of her affair with John Proctor.

**Reverend Hale** Minister in Beverly. The people of Salem summon him to investigate Betty's condition and determine if witchcraft is responsible. He supports the witch trials, but later denounces them when he learns that Abigail is lying.

**Rebecca Nurse** Wife of Francis Nurse. She is one of the most respected individuals in Salem because of her kindness and charity. She argues against the witch trial investigations. Mrs. Putnam accuses her of witchcraft.

**Francis Nurse** Farmer and landowner in Salem. He is a respected member of the community often called upon to settle disagreements between individuals.

**Susanna Walcott** Friend to Abigail. She also takes part in the trials by falsely accusing others of witchcraft.

**Giles Corey** Elderly inhabitant of Salem. He challenges the court in an attempt to defend his wife who has been convicted of witchcraft. He is pressed to death as a result.

**Sarah Good** Beggar in Salem. She is the first individual accused of witchcraft.

**Judge Hathorne** A judge in the Salem court.

**Deputy Governor Danforth** A special judge serving in the Salem court during the witch trials. He signs the death sentences for those individuals who refuse to confess their crimes. He refuses to delay any execution for fear that he will appear weak and irresolute.

**Ezekial Cheever** Appointed by the court to assist in arresting accused individuals.

**Marshal Herrick** Appointed by the court to arrest the accused individuals.

**Hopkins** Jailer.

# Character Web

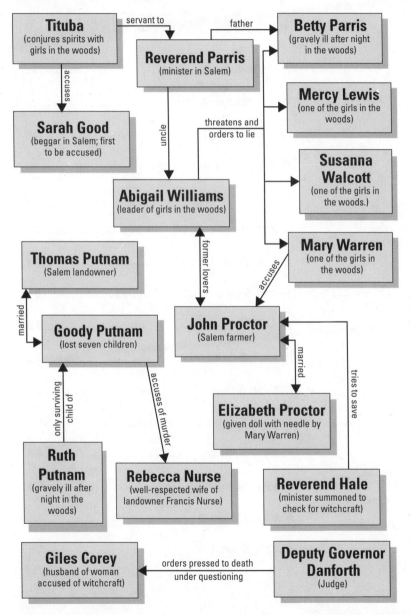

**Tituba**
(conjures spirits with girls in the woods)

*servant to* →

*father* →

**Betty Parris**
(gravely ill after night in the woods)

**Reverend Parris**
(minister in Salem)

*accuses*

**Mercy Lewis**
(one of the girls in the woods)

**Sarah Good**
(beggar in Salem; first to be accused)

*uncle*

*threatens and orders to lie*

**Susanna Walcott**
(one of the girls in the woods.)

**Abigail Williams**
(leader of girls in the woods)

**Mary Warren**
(one of the girls in the woods)

**Thomas Putnam**
(Salem landowner)

*former lovers*

*accuses*

*married*

**Goody Putnam**
(lost seven children)

**John Proctor**
(Salem farmer)

*married*

*tries to save*

*only surviving child of*

*accuses of murder*

**Elizabeth Proctor**
(given doll with needle by Mary Warren)

**Ruth Putnam**
(gravely ill after night in the woods)

**Rebecca Nurse**
(well-respected wife of landowner Francis Nurse)

**Reverend Hale**
(minister summoned to check for witchcraft)

**Giles Corey**
(husband of woman accused of witchcraft)

*orders pressed to death under questioning* ←

**Deputy Governor Danforth**
(Judge)

# CRITICAL COMMENTARIES

# Act I
# Scene 1

## Summary

*The Crucible* begins in the house of Reverend Samuel Parris, whose daughter, Betty, lies unconscious in bed upstairs. Prior to the opening of the play, Parris discovered Betty, his niece Abigail, and Tituba, his black slave from Barbados, dancing in the forest outside of Salem at midnight. After Parris came out of the bushes, Betty lost consciousness and has remained in a stupor ever since. The town physician, Doctor Griggs, who has not been able to determine why Betty is ill, suggests witchcraft as a possible cause.

Parris, distraught and troubled because he knows that Abigail has not been entirely truthful regarding her activities in the woods, confronts Abigail. Parris says that he saw her and Betty dancing "like heathen[s]," Tituba moving back and forth over a fire while mumbling unintelligibly, and an unidentified female running naked through the forest. Abigail denies that she and the other girls were participating in witchcraft, but Parris suspects she is lying. He thinks that she and Betty have conjured spells. Parris also questions Abigail about her character and the reason why Goody Proctor, who is the wife of John Proctor and a very respected woman in Salem, dismissed her from working as the Proctors' servant.

Mr. and Mrs. Putnam, members of one of the prominent families in Salem, enter the room and declare that Betty's illness results from witchcraft. They reveal to Parris that their daughter, Ruth, has also fallen into a strange trance. Ruth's condition, coupled with the fact that seven of Mrs. Putnam's children have died as infants under mysterious conditions, convince the Putnams that evil spirits are at work in Salem. Putnam tries to persuade Parris that he should declare the presence of witchcraft, but Parris is worried. He knows that a group of townspeople want to remove him from Salem, and a witchcraft scandal involving his family would give them the power to oust him from the town.

# Commentary

The inhabitants of Salem live in an extremely restrictive society. Although the Puritans left England to avoid religious persecution, they established a society in America founded upon religious intolerance. Government and religious authority are virtually inseparable, and individuals who question local authority are accused of questioning divine authority. The Puritan community considered physical labor and strict adherence to religious doctrine the best indicators of faithfulness, honesty, and integrity. The Puritans considered material and sexual desires unnatural and evil, and a threat to society. Salem was a rigid society that emphasized work and the suppression of individual desires.

**Theme**

**Literary Device**

In Act I, Scene 1, Miller sets the stage for *The Crucible* by introducing the four most important themes: deception, possession, greed, and the quest for power.

The "unseen" scene in the woods, which takes place before the action of the play, figuratively sets the stage. This scene serves as a catalyst for the remaining action of the play. Parris informs Abigail that he saw girls dancing, Tituba conjuring spells over the fire, and a naked girl running through the woods. This "unseen" scene symbolizes the suppression of desire, which is paramount in Salem. Desire, of course, has many different interpretations for both the characters within the play, and for the audience. For Abigail, desire refers to her sexual longing for Proctor. According to the other characters, and the audience, desire may mean many other things besides sexual longing. For example, Putnam desires land and Parris desires control and authority. The audience, inevitably, will have other interpretations of this concept.

Because the girls cannot dance within Salem, they must retreat into the woods outside of Salem in order to indulge in physical pleasure. In addition, the naked girl running through the woods symbolizes the sexual desire present in all of the inhabitants of Salem, a desire that society forces them to suppress and negate. In order to express their innate desires (whether innocent or not), the girls must go outside of the community into the wilderness. Religion has not tamed the forests or the heathen Indians that inhabit them, so the Puritans view the woods as the Devil's stronghold. The wilderness outside of Salem is comparable to the wilderness in which Satan tempted Jesus. Although Jesus did not succumb to temptation, Satan led him into the wilderness to entice him to sin. The girls actively seek the wilderness because it provides them with a place where they can exercise desires that society considers unacceptable.

# Glossary

(Here and in the following sections, difficult words and phrases are explained.)

**crucible** a container made of a substance that can resist great heat, for melting, fusing, or calcining ores, metals, and the like; a severe test or trial; here, meaning a test designed to bring about change or reveal an individual's true character.

**parochial** of or in a parish or parishes; restricted to a small area or scope; narrow; limited; provincial; here, referring to the narrow-mindedness of the inhabitants of Salem.

**autocracy** a government in which one person has absolute power; dictatorship; despotism.

**theocracy** a government by a person or persons claiming to rule with divine authority.

**paradox** a statement that seems contradictory, unbelievable, or absurd but that may be true in fact. For example, the Puritans created a theocracy in order to provide a unified and stable community in Salem. Instead, the witch trials severed social relations, separated families, and turned the people of Salem against one another.

**dissemble** to conceal under a false appearance; disguise.

**Goody** [Archaic] a woman, esp. an old woman or housewife, of lowly social status: used as a title with the surname.

**providence** the care or benevolent guidance of God or nature; here, the meaning is more closely aligned with "godsend," an unexpected but fortunate event. For example, Putnam believes God has revealed the presence of witchcraft in Salem. Although the idea of witchcraft frightens Putnam, he is grateful that the witchcraft has been revealed while it is still possible to control it.

**conjure up** to raise spirits from the dead.

# Act I
# Scene 2

## Summary

Abigail and Mercy, the Putnams' servant, try to wake Betty. Abigail tells Mercy what to say when she is questioned about what she was doing in the woods. She informs Mercy that Parris knows they were dancing in the woods. She also says he knows Tituba called to Ruth's dead sisters. Abigail reveals that Mercy is the female that Parris saw running naked through the woods.

Mary Warren enters the room and tells Abigail that everyone in Salem blames witchcraft for Betty's illness. The idea that the townspeople will label her and the other girls witches frightens and worries Marry Warren. The three girls begin to argue and Betty wakes.

Abigail tells Betty that Parris knows everything they did in the woods. Betty confronts Abigail and accuses her of not admitting she drank blood. She also accuses her of casting a spell in order to kill Goody Proctor. Threatening to practice witchcraft on Betty, Mercy, and Mary Warren if they tell anyone about the spell, Abigail tells them to say that they only danced, that Tituba raised Ruth's sisters from the dead, and that nothing else happened. Betty collapses again in a stupor.

## Commentary

**Theme**

As the action of the play begins, the girls' behavior in the woods introduces deception as a major theme. Abigail is the instigator. Whereas the other girls may have participated in the rituals out of curiosity, Abigail has a definite agenda. She has experienced sexual pleasure with John Proctor and now wants to kill Proctor's wife, Elizabeth. Abigail realizes that the Puritanical society will never permit Proctor to leave his wife for her, and that he does not want to leave his wife anyway. The only way that Abigail can legitimately obtain Proctor within the bounds of society is for Elizabeth to die, giving Proctor the opportunity to marry again. Thus, from the very beginning, Abigail's desire to possess Proctor motivates her, driving her to drink blood and cast a spell on Elizabeth. Once Parris discovers her in the woods, Abigail resorts to deception in order to prevent others from discovering that she practiced witchcraft and to hide her affair with Proctor. Either one of these offenses would result in severe punishment at the hands of society.

**Character Insight**

Abigail uses intimidation to create an atmosphere of fear that pervades the entire play. Abigail first demonstrates her penchant for terrorizing others in her threat to the girls: "Let either of you breathe a word, or the edge of a word, about the other things, and I will come to you in the black of some terrible night and I will bring a pointy reckoning that will shudder you . . . I can make you wish you had never seen the sun go down!" This threat foreshadows Abigail's accusations of witchcraft against others. Just as she threatens to harm the other girls through conjurings and witchcraft if they do not do as she says, so Abigail later carefully eliminates her enemies by accusing them of witchcraft. What begins as a simple act of self-preservation quickly turns into an opportunity to achieve power—and, ultimately, John Proctor.

## Glossary

**grand peeping courage** behavior or attribute of someone who is too frightened to participate in a ritual, but will watch others participate.

**pointy reckoning** the act or process of getting even or getting revenge.

# Act I
# Scene 3

## Summary

John Proctor and Abigail are alone in the room with Betty. Proctor questions Abigail about Betty's illness, suspecting that responsibility for "this mischief" probably lies with Abigail. Denying any involvement in witchcraft, Abigail states that she and the girls merely danced in the woods.

Abigail asks Proctor if he has come to see her, but Proctor denies it. The conversation reveals that approximately seven months earlier, Abigail and Proctor had an affair while Abigail lived and worked in the Proctor household. Goody Proctor subsequently dismissed Abigail. Now Abigail accuses Proctor of still being in love with her, even though he will not admit it to her or himself.

## Commentary

Character
Insight

Abigail is the exact opposite of Proctor's morally upright wife, Elizabeth. Abigail represents the repressed desires—sexual, material, or other—possessed by all of the Puritans. The difference between Abigail and the other residents of Salem is that she does not suppress her desires. Abigail goes after what she wants and uses any means to achieve her goal, even manipulation, deception, and seduction.

While Abigail lived with the Proctors, Elizabeth was very ill. Abigail's responsibilities expanded and she began to see herself taking Elizabeth's place as Mrs. John Proctor. Not surprisingly, Proctor, lonely and vulnerable, noticed Abigail and became attracted to her. She was more visible in the house and interacted with him more than Elizabeth. However, the key to Proctor's desire for Abigail is her willingness to discard Puritan social restrictions. Whereas another Puritan woman would have concealed her desire for a married man, Abigail instead tempted Proctor and eventually enticed him to sin.

Scene 3 performs a pivotal role in the play because it reveals Abigail's only vulnerability: her feelings for John Proctor. Because Betty lies unconscious, Abigail seizes the opportunity to speak with Proctor alone and reaffirm their relationship. Although Proctor remains resolute in his decision not to become involved with Abigail again, she and her blatant impropriety still captivate him. The thought of Abigail and the others dancing in the woods amuses and excites Proctor because society forbids the acts. Abigail interprets Proctor's reaction to her "wicked" behavior as a sign that he still cares for her. When Proctor refuses to admit any feelings for Abigail or to even speak of their affair, Abigail grows angry and blames Elizabeth for his indifference.

Proctor's determination to remain faithful to Elizabeth establishes his character's morals, and provides Abigail with her sole motivation throughout the remainder of the play. Prior to Scene 3, Abigail views Elizabeth as an inconvenience because she is preventing Abigail from being with Proctor. Now, however, Abigail sees Elizabeth as a threat because Proctor no longer acknowledges his feelings for Abigail. Up until this point in the play, Abigail's only concern has been concealing her behavior in the woods and her affair with Proctor. Now Abigail knows that she must deal with Elizabeth or lose Proctor completely. This realization foreshadows Abigail's actions in Scene 5.

# Glossary

**partisan**  a person who takes the part of or strongly supports one side, party, or person; often, specifically, an unreasoning, emotional adherent.

**faction**  a group of people inside a political party, club, government, and so on, working in a common cause against other such groups or against the main body; here, it refers to those resisting Reverend Parris.

**calumny**  a false and malicious statement meant to hurt someone's reputation.

**soft**  gentle; low; not loud or harsh: said of sound.

**sportin'**  jesting; joking.

**wintry**  of or like winter; cold, bleak; Here, it means without feeling.

**covenant** a binding and solemn agreement to do or keep from doing a specified thing; compact; the promise made by God to humanity, as described in the Bible. Here, "covenanted" specifically refers to a person bound by God's law and scriptures. For example, John Proctor is a married man and is bound to Elizabeth through their marriage promise or contract. According to God's law, Proctor and Elizabeth must remain faithful to one another. Of course, the entire premise of *The Crucible* is the result of Proctor's and Abigail's infidelity.

# Act I
# Scene 4

## Summary

Betty begins screaming and covering her ears. Parishioners downstairs have been singing a hymn. Mrs. Putnam interprets Betty's behavior as a sign of witchcraft because "she cannot bear to hear the Lord's name!" Rebecca Nurse instructs everyone to be quiet and then stands by Betty until she calms down.

Putnam asks Rebecca to visit Ruth and attempt to wake her. Rebecca tells Putnam and the others that Betty and Ruth's condition will pass, and she warns Parris that looking to witchcraft would be a dangerous explanation of the girls' behavior. Putnam declares that witchcraft is to blame for the loss of his seven infant children, and Mrs. Putnam becomes hostile to Rebecca. She is suspicious because Rebecca has not lost any of her children.

Proctor criticizes Parris for preaching about money rather than God. Putnam, Proctor, and Giles Corey argue with Parris about his salary and his expectations as the minister of Salem. Parris claims that a faction within Salem is determined to get rid of him. The men begin discussing lawsuits and land rights. Putnam accuses Proctor of stealing wood from his land, but Proctor says he bought the land five months before from Goody Nurse's husband. Putnam states that Goody Nurse's husband did not own the land because it belonged to Putnam's grandfather. Proctor counters Putnam.

## Commentary

Scene 4 reveals old animosities that later drive the action of the play. In this time period, it was not uncommon for children to die at birth or early in childhood for a number of reasons, including poor medical treatment, improper nutrition, and harsh living conditions. Even so, seven is an unusually high number of children's deaths within one family, and losing seven children, coupled with the threat to her surviving child, has left Mrs. Putnam a bitter woman. Inherently self-righteous, she believes she has been victimized and devotes all of her energy to discovering the cause of her children's deaths. Mrs. Putnam's obsession not only leads her to solicit Tituba's services in conjuring her children's spirits, but also results in jealousy toward other mothers who have not lost children. In this case, Mrs. Putnam focuses her jealousy and animosity upon Rebecca Nurse because Rebecca never lost one of her eleven children. Mrs. Putnam's anger toward Rebecca foreshadows Rebecca's arrest just before Act II, Scene 3. Mrs. Putnam may not have learned from Tituba why her children were born dead, but through the witch trials Mrs. Putnam manages to carry out her vengeance and anger by accusing Rebecca, an individual who has what she has always wanted.

**Theme**

Scene 4 also introduces greed and the quest for power or authority as the two other major themes of the play. Parris' argument with Proctor and Corey reveals that money causes many disputes within Salem. Tension arises when Proctor accuses Parris of concerning himself more with material gain than ministering to the inhabitants of Salem.

Proctor's anger is consistent with his character because he lives according to the morals and work ethic described in the Bible. This does not mean Proctor is perfect. His adulterous affair with Abigail presents a major flaw, but Proctor recognizes his sin and suffers greatly under the weight of his guilt. Parris' haggling over his contract, salary, and provisions disgusts Proctor. Proctor believes a minister obsessed with obtaining material goods—such as golden candlesticks, rather than pewter ones—cannot truly serve God or minister to others.

**Character Insight**

On the other hand, one can understand Parris' concern over job security. Proctor criticizes Parris' request for the deed to his home, but Parris is acting reasonably because he knows Salem's history of getting rid of ministers. Once a very successful businessman in Barbados, lifestyle and economic expectations changed dramatically when he became a minister; however, Parris continues to think like a secular individual. He is used to material goods, such as the gold candlesticks mentioned in Act II, Scene 3, and he is accustomed to examining all of his options. Just as a resourceful businessman investigates all possible outcomes of a business deal, so Parris attempts to cover himself just in case things do not work out in Salem. Asking for the deed to his home not only decreases the possibility of a faction removing him from the pulpit, but it provides a place for him and his family if such an event actually occurs.

Parris' argument with Proctor also symbolizes Parris' continual battle to obtain authority within Salem. Parris views Proctor as his primary opponent, demonstrated when he accuses Proctor of leading a faction against him. Parris' anger stems from the fact that he feels that the inhabitants of Salem fail to recognize his authority when they refuse to acknowledge their "obligations toward the ministry." Just as Mrs. Putnam targets Rebecca because she is in the room and she is one of the mothers who has not lost a child, so Parris targets Proctor because he is there in front of him and, therefore, representative of the other undutiful inhabitants of Salem.

**Literary
Device**

The end of Scene 4 reveals other animosities when Proctor and Putnam begin arguing over land rights. Proctor goes to leave and states that he must haul lumber back to his home. Putnam accuses Proctor of stealing wood from his land, even though Proctor states that he had purchased the land from Francis Nurse five months prior. Just as Scene 3 results in a new reason for Abigail to accuse others of witchcraft, so Scene 4 provides the Putnams with a lucrative motivation to accuse their neighbors of witchcraft. After Scene 3, Abigail's purpose is to accuse Elizabeth and obtain Proctor for herself. After Scene 4, the Putnams' purpose is to accuse anyone who "took" land that they believe should be theirs. Again, this shift foreshadows the arrest of Rebecca, as well as Martha Corey and numerous others in Act II.

## Glossary

**prodigious**  notable; here, meaning ominous.

**arbitrate**  to act as an impartial judge in order to settle disputes.

**silly season**  phrase used to describe unexplainable, but natural behavior for a child.

**bewildered**  confused or disoriented; here, meaning bewitched or acting unnaturally.

**wheels within wheels . . . fires within fires**  phrase used to imply conspiracies.

**defamation**  damaging another individual's character or reputation, generally through false accusations.

## Act I
# Scene 5

## Summary

Reverend Hale arrives at Parris' house. Hale tells Rebecca Nurse that people in his town know her good deeds well. The Putnams describe Ruth's condition to Hale and ask him to examine her, but first Hale prepares to look at Betty. Hale tells everyone in the room that he will not examine Betty unless they accept the fact that witchcraft may not be the reason for her ailment: "I shall not proceed unless you are prepared to believe me if I should find no bruise of Hell upon her."

Mrs. Putnam states that Tituba can conjure spirits. Mrs. Putnam admits that she sent Ruth to Tituba so that Tituba could conjure Ruth's dead sisters in order to find out who murdered them.

Goody Nurse leaves when Hale prepares to examine Betty for signs of the Devil because Hale says the process may cause the child pain. Giles Corey tells Hale that his wife Martha has been secretly reading books and that these books prevent him from praying.

Parris tells Hale about Abigail, Betty, and the others dancing in the woods. Hale questions Abigail, and she blames Tituba for everything. Abigail says that Tituba makes her drink blood, plagues her dreams, and tempts her to sin.

Hale questions Tituba and tells her that she can redeem herself by admitting that she has been working with the Devil and by telling him the names of anyone else involved. She admits that she has seen the Devil and that Goody Good and Goody Osburn were with him.

Abigail admits that she has given herself to the Devil by writing her name in his book. She renounces the Devil and says that she wants "the sweet love of Jesus." Abigail also claims to have seen Goody Good and Goody Osburn with the Devil, along with Bridget Bishop. Betty wakes up and claims that she saw George Jacobs and Goody Howe with the Devil. Act I ends with Abigail and Betty naming individuals that they have seen with the Devil.

# Commentary

**Literary Device**

Scene 5 is pivotal in the play for two reasons. First, this scene establishes the expectation of witchcraft in Salem. Hale warns everyone in the room that he will not examine Betty unless they acknowledge the fact that witchcraft may *not* be involved. Although everyone agrees, they overwhelmingly expect and hope that he will discover witchcraft. The idea of discovering witchcraft in one's own backyard is not only exciting, but it allows individuals to find an explanation for things that they otherwise cannot explain. For example, Mrs. Putnam's blaming her children's deaths upon witchcraft is easier than admitting that she did not give birth to healthy children, or that she cannot carry children successfully. Explaining that Betty and Ruth's ailments result from witchcraft is also much easier than admitting that good Puritan girls were out dancing in the woods and attempting to cast spells and are now feigning illness to avoid punishment.

Even though Hale states a disclaimer at the beginning of Scene 5, nearly everyone expects him to find evidence of witchcraft; they will not be satisfied unless he does. As a result, Hale is overcome by the many descriptions of all of the unnatural events occurring in Salem: Betty's illness, Ruth's condition, Tituba's ability to conjure spirits, dancing in the woods, the death of the seven Putnam children, Martha Corey's strange books, and so forth. He might explain any one of these events in isolation, but together, they serve as overwhelming evidence of witchcraft in Salem.

Mrs. Putnam's anger toward Rebecca only intensifies when Rebecca criticizes her for sending Ruth to conjure up the dead with Tituba. Under normal circumstances, the Puritans would severely punish Mrs. Putnam for her actions, because they considered attempting to contact the dead and endangering the life of a child the Devil's work. However, Mrs. Putnam not only avoids punishment, but she manipulates Rebecca's reaction and her refusal to stay during Hale's examination of Betty as proof of Rebecca's involvement in the witchcraft.

**Character Insight**

The second reason that Scene 5 is pivotal is because Abigail exerts her power and begins her quest to obtain Proctor. Unsurprisingly, Tituba confesses to witchcraft when the townspeople threaten her with physical violence. She is a black female slave, an individual without any power. She cannot hope to defend herself against Abigail's accusations, even though she and Abigail both know that Abigail is lying.

The fact that Tituba confesses to witchcraft and then implicates Sarah Good and Goody Osburn reveals that Tituba listens very well and values her life. In order to preserve her own life, Tituba takes cues from her interrogators and tells them what they want to hear. Hale's response to Tituba's confession prompts Abigail's own sudden admission of guilt.

**Character Insight**

Declaring witchcraft becomes the popular thing to do. It grants an individual instant status and recognition within Salem, which translates into power. Abigail realizes that she can achieve immediate respect and authority by declaring that she has consorted with the Devil but now seeks redemption. Abigail's manipulation of the circumstances demonstrates her keen sense of self-preservation, as well as a unique understanding of the blind ignorance of others. Abigail knows that the townspeople will view her as an expert witness. The fact that Hale believes her sets her far apart from the other people in Salem. The people forget Abigail's questionable reputation and now consider her an instrument of God. This calculated move finally puts her in a position to get rid of Elizabeth Proctor. The fact that Betty suddenly awakens after Abigail renounces the Devil only underscores Abigail's authority and further establishes her credibility.

## Glossary

**diabolism** dealings with the Devil or devils, as by sorcery or witchcraft.

**inculcate** to impress upon the mind by frequent repetition or persistent urging.

**licentious** morally unrestrained, esp. in sexual activity; lascivious.

**truck** the practice of bartering; [Informal] dealings (have no further *truck* with them). Here, also a verb, meaning to be in league with someone. For example Tituba denies trucking, or being in league with, the Devil.

# Act II
# Scene 1

## Summary

Act II begins in the house of John Proctor eight days after Abigail and Betty began accusing individuals of witchcraft. Proctor returns late after working in the fields and eats dinner with his wife Elizabeth. Proctor tells Elizabeth that he is striving to make her happy.

Elizabeth questions Proctor to find out if he was late for dinner because he had gone to Salem. She tells Proctor that their servant, Mary Warren, has been in Salem all day. Proctor becomes angry because he told Mary Warren not to go to Salem. Elizabeth tells Proctor that Mary Warren has been named an official of the court. Proctor learns that four magistrates have been named to the General Court and the Deputy Governor of the Province is serving as the judge. The court has jailed fourteen people for witchcraft.

Elizabeth tells Proctor that he must go to Salem and reveal that Abigail is a fake. Proctor hesitates and then reveals that he cannot prove what Abigail said because they were alone when they talked. Elizabeth becomes upset with Proctor because he did not tell her he spent time alone with Abigail. Proctor and Elizabeth argue. Proctor is angry because he believes Elizabeth is accusing him of dishonesty and is suspicious that he has resumed his affair with Abigail. Elizabeth is angry because she does not believe Proctor is completely honest with her.

## Commentary

Act II, Scene 1 provides the audience with the first glimpse of Elizabeth and John Proctor together. Up until this point, the audience has only heard about Elizabeth through Abigail and Proctor. Abigail has described Elizabeth as a cold "sniveling" woman who cannot possibly satisfy Proctor or make him happy. Proctor has vehemently defended Elizabeth.

From outward appearances, the Proctor household seems to be the typical Puritan home. As Proctor and Elizabeth eat dinner they discuss the farm, crops, and domestic issues; however, tension exists in the house. Elizabeth knows about Proctor's affair. She tells Proctor that she forgives him, but a lingering distrust plagues her. Even though Proctor has remained faithful for the past seven months and is truly sorry for his affair, Elizabeth faces difficulty moving beyond the past. As a result, Proctor feels that Elizabeth continually scrutinizes his actions, which frustrates and angers him.

**Character Insight**

Tension and mutual frustration define their relationship. Elizabeth is frustrated with Proctor because of his initial infidelity and because she believes he still has feelings for Abigail. She is also frustrated with herself. She wants to forgive Proctor and begin reestablishing their relationship, but she cannot forget what he has done. Elizabeth tries to demonstrate her faith in Proctor when she asks him to go to Salem even though she does not want him anywhere near Abigail. However, the fact that he spent time alone with Abigail shatters Elizabeth's confidence in him. Elizabeth automatically suspects Proctor of wrongdoing.

Proctor, however, regrets his affair with Abigail. His own guilt, coupled with Elizabeth's subtle recrimination, wearies him. He too would like to move beyond the past and strengthen their marriage, but he does not know how to deal with Elizabeth's feelings or the distance between them. During the past seven months, Proctor has tried to please Elizabeth to gain her forgiveness and affection, but nothing seems to work. The current argument over Abigail is yet another example of their strained relationship. He is irritated with himself because he did not tell Elizabeth he was alone with Abigail in the first place. Now, Elizabeth is angry, not just because he was alone with Abigail, but because he did not tell her from the beginning.

## Glossary

**clapped** put, moved, set swiftly ( *clapped* into jail).

**your justice would freeze beer** said here to a person who forgives another for an injustice, but still harbors resentment for the deed and makes the other person feel guilty.

# Act II
# Scene 2

## Summary

Mary Warren returns to the Proctor house. Proctor is furious that she has been in Salem all day, but Mary Warren tells him she will be gone every day because she is an official of the court. Mary Warren gives Elizabeth a poppet that she made while in court. Mary Warren tells Elizabeth and Proctor that thirty-nine people are in jail, and Goody Osburn will hang because she did not confess to witchcraft. Proctor becomes angry because he believes the court is condemning people without solid evidence. Mary Warren states that Elizabeth was accused, but she defended Elizabeth and the court dismissed the accusation.

Elizabeth tells Proctor that Abigail wants to get rid of her. Elizabeth believes that Abigail will accuse her of witchcraft and then have her executed. Elizabeth realizes that Abigail wants to take her place as Proctor's wife. Elizabeth asks Proctor to speak to Abigail and tell her that no chance exists of Proctor marrying her if something happened to Elizabeth. Elizabeth and Proctor argue again.

## Commentary

Theme

Scene 2 reveals the impact of the witch trials and the frenzy they have created in Salem, reinforcing the theme of how easily a mob can be influenced. Suddenly the townspeople revere the youth of the town, namely Abigail and the other girls, as instruments of God. Anyone who has crossed the girls lives in fear of being accused of witchcraft.

As the leader of the group, Abigail has finally achieved the power she desires, and now she can use it to obtain Proctor. The other girls have achieved new status as well. Prior to the witch trials, Mary Warren lived as a servant in the Proctor home. She was paid for her services, but she was also under the authority of Proctor and was required to follow the rules of the house. If Mary Warren did not fulfill her work obligations, Proctor could discipline her just like one of the Proctor children. This type of arrangement was acceptable and normal within Puritan society.

After the witch trials begin, the social hierarchy of Salem becomes unstable. Individuals who previously did not have power obtain it and refuse to submit to others who traditionally have authority over them. Mary Warren provides a clear demonstration of this when she refuses to take orders from Elizabeth and stands up to Proctor when he threatens to whip her for insubordination.

**Character Insight**

In Scene 2 Mary Warren begins to cry. Serving on the court all day has exhausted and upset her. At this point, Mary Warren attempts to convince herself and the Proctors that solid evidence exists against all of the accused. She secretly questions this, but feels she can only go along with Abigail and the others. She now belongs to a group, and does not want to be an outcast.

**Literary Device**

Abigail's scheme becomes apparent to Elizabeth and Proctor within Scene 2. This is central to the play because, up until this point, only the audience knows what is really happening. Now two of the characters accurately interpret Abigail's actions and her overall objective. Before Scene 2, Proctor and Elizabeth knew that Abigail had lied about the witchcraft incident, and both suspected that Abigail wanted to get rid of Elizabeth. Scene 2 confirms their fears. The poppet that Mary Warren innocently gives to Elizabeth foreshadows Elizabeth's arrest in Scene 4.

When Mary Warren tells them the court accused Elizabeth, Abigail's plan becomes clear. Time is now the most important element in the play. With each arrest for witchcraft, Abigail gains credibility. In addition, the courtroom fits, trances, fainting spells, and other demonstrations of "hard evidence" increase Abigail's authority. She is quickly becoming irrefutable in the eyes of the court.

Proctor only has two chances to save Elizabeth. Either he must speak to Abigail and convince her that her plan will not work, or he must speak to Hale before Abigail accuses Elizabeth. If Proctor calls Abigail a fraud after Elizabeth's arrest, he will appear to be lashing out. Proctor must act as quickly as possible because both Proctor and Elizabeth know that Abigail will continue to accuse Elizabeth until the court arrests her.

## Glossary

**poppet** [Obsolete] a doll.

**hard proof** undeniable, reliable, or actual proof; here, the phrase refers to solid evidence.

**base** having or showing little or no honor, courage, or decency; mean; ignoble; contemptible.

# Act II
# Scene 3

## Summary

Reverend Hale visits the Proctor house. Hale tells Elizabeth and Proctor that Elizabeth was named in court. Hale questions Proctor about his poor attendance in church. Hale asks Proctor to recite the Ten Commandments. Proctor can only recall nine and Elizabeth reminds him of the one he forgot—the commandment forbidding adultery. The fact that Proctor forgets this particular commandment is not unintentional. Irony is created here because the audience, along with Proctor and Elizabeth, realizes that he really "forgot" the commandment when he had the affair with Abigail. Proctor has not incorporated this commandment into his life, so it fails to remain in his memory.

Proctor tells Hale that Abigail admitted to him that witchcraft was not responsible for the children's ailments. Hale asks Proctor to testify in court that Abigail is a fraud. Hale then questions Elizabeth to find out if she believes in witches. Giles Corey and Francis Nurse arrive and tell Proctor, Hale, and Elizabeth that the court has arrested both Martha Corey and Rebecca Nurse for witchcraft.

## Commentary

Hale is a fair individual who honestly attempts to administer justice. He remains uninvolved in the petty rivalries and power plays of the inhabitants of Salem. Several issues disturb Hale and make him suspicious of the Proctors. These include Proctor's poor church attendance, the fact that one of the Proctor children remains unbaptized, and Proctor's inability to recite all of the Ten Commandments. He comes to the Proctor home on his own in order to test the Proctors and give them fair warning of Elizabeth's possible arrest.

**Character Insight**

The fact that Hale gives Proctor the opportunity to explain each of the incriminating items is an important testament to Hale's fairness and directly contrasts with what happened in Act I, Scene 5. In Act I, Scene 5, the inhabitants of Salem provide a list of evidence that Hale takes at face value and fails to analyze individually. As a result, Hale declares witchcraft without attempting to examine any of the evidence.

Here, however, Hale allows Proctor to explain his actions. Although Hale disapproves of Proctor's actions—particularly his refusal to baptize his son because of feelings toward Parris—Hale realizes that Proctor is not an evil man.

Tension also arises in Scene 3 between the Proctors and Hale over issues of faith. Both Elizabeth and Proctor refuse to believe that Rebecca could be involved with witchcraft, and the accusation horrifies them both. Although Hale is hesitant to believe that Rebecca could be guilty, he will not dismiss the possibility.

At this point the play introduces the issue of an individual's works. The Puritans looked to the Scriptures as a guide for daily life. They did not believe that faith was a sufficient indication of religious dedication, unless a person demonstrated that faith through good deeds. Not surprisingly, the Proctors argue with Hale over Rebecca, considering her history of good works. Hale seems willing to discount Rebecca's past works, even though Puritan ministers preach that God judges people according to their works.

Hale extends this argument when he questions Elizabeth regarding whether or not she believes in witches. Elizabeth denies the fact that witches exist because of Hale's attitude toward Rebecca. Elizabeth does not believe that Rebecca can possibly be a witch because the idea contradicts the morality of the Scriptures. Elizabeth knows that suspicion hangs over her also. Elizabeth has devoted her life to moral goodness and charity; therefore, she refuses to acknowledge the existence of witches when the court could label her as one.

Proctor's statement that Abigail admitted she was faking the entire witchcraft incident forces Hale to reexamine his own faith and actions in the preceding events. Hale realizes that good intentions and a firm commitment to God governed his own actions. However, he also realizes that he may have imprisoned innocent people and condemned to death those individuals who refused to confess to something they did not do.

## Glossary

**trafficked**  had traffic, trade, or dealings with.

**softness**  the quality of being easily impressed, influenced, or imposed upon; here, lax or negligent.

**bound**  under compulsion; obliged; here it means in service to.

**tainted**  morally corrupt.

# Act II
# Scene 4

## Summary

Ezekiel Cheever and Marshal Herrick arrive at the Proctor house with a warrant for Elizabeth's arrest. Cheever discovers the poppet that Mary Warren made for Elizabeth, and he finds a needle inside the doll. Cheever tells Proctor and Hale that Abigail has charged Elizabeth with attempted murder. Cheever says that Abigail was stabbed with a needle while eating at Parris' house, and Abigail accused Elizabeth's spirit of stabbing her.

Mary Warren tells Hale that she made the doll in court that day and stored the needle inside the doll. Mary Warren also states that Abigail saw her sewing because she sat next to Mary Warren. The men still take Elizabeth into custody, and Hale, Corey, and Nurse leave.

Proctor tells Mary Warren that she must testify in court against Abigail. Mary Warren tells Proctor that she fears testifying against Abigail because Abigail and the others will turn against her. Proctor discovers that Mary Warren knows about his affair.

## Commentary

Abigail begins to execute her plan against Elizabeth in Scene 4. At this point Abigail exercises all of the power she has gained from the beginning of the play. Abigail realizes that in order to have Elizabeth arrested, she will have to create tangible evidence for the court, because it dismissed her verbal accusation. She is prepared to do anything to charge Elizabeth with witchcraft.

**Character Insight**

Abigail realizes that she can use Mary Warren as a tool to incriminate Elizabeth, and so she constructs a plot based upon deception and manipulation of Mary Warren. Abigail has seen Mary Warren sewing the poppet in court and she knows that Mary Warren will give the doll to Elizabeth later. The fact that Abigail willingly inflicts a stabbing wound upon herself demonstrates how far she will go to destroy Elizabeth and possess Proctor.

Scene 4 also provides Proctor with an opportunity to discredit Abigail and prove the falsity of her accusation against Elizabeth. The problem is whether or not Mary Warren will testify against Abigail in open court. She admits that the poppet is her own and that Abigail saw her sewing it, and had even seen her store the needle inside. However, Mary Warren would not reveal this if Hale questioned her in order to disprove Abigail's claim. To save Elizabeth, Mary Warren must give up her sense of belonging, and face Abigail's initial threat of violence from Act I, Scene 2.

**Literary Device**

Mary Warren's fear of reprisal foreshadows Abigail's behavior toward Mary Warren in Act III. In addition, Mary Warren warns Proctor that Abigail will accuse him of adultery. This foreshadows the end of the play when Proctor reveals the affair in court.

# Glossary

**tonnage**  weight in tons.

**calamity**  deep trouble or misery; any extreme misfortune bringing great loss and sorrow; disaster.

**broken**  sick, weakened, or beaten; here, meaning weak and imperfect.

**as clean as God's fingers**  pure or perfect, in the way that all parts of God are flawless.

**lechery**  unrestrained, excessive indulgence of sexual desires; gross sensuality; lewdness; here, lechery refers to Proctor's affair with Abigail.

# Act III
# Scene 1

## Summary

Act III begins in the Salem meeting house. The court questions and accuses Martha Corey of witchcraft. Giles Corey interrupts the court proceedings and declares that Thomas Putnam is "reaching out for land!" He is removed from the courtroom and taken to the vestry room.

Judge Hathorne, Deputy Governor Danforth, Ezekiel Cheever, and Parris enter the vestry room. Corey says that he owns six hundred acres of land, and a large quantity of timber. Corey also states that the court is holding his wife Martha by mistake. Corey tells Danforth that he had asked Hale why Martha read books, but he never accused her of witchcraft.

Corey and Francis Nurse state that they both have evidence for the court. They have been waiting for three days to present the evidence, but to no avail. Danforth responds that they must file the appropriate paperwork for the court to hear them. Nurse tells Danforth the girls are pretending.

## Commentary

Time plays a critical role in Act III. The fascination with witchcraft that appeared in Act I, Scene 5 has quickly changed to mass paranoia. The townspeople now regard anyone who does not conform exactly to the laws of Salem society as a potential witch. Fear and automatic suspicion replace reason. As the power of the court grows, the people of Salem live in fear. Old grudges, dislikes, and minor misdeeds can result in arrest and death—especially if the person offended is one of the children in the town, or someone who seeks more land. As the number of arrests increases, the court shows no mercy and refuses to acknowledge the idea that the accusers may have hidden agendas.

Not surprisingly, Proctor, Giles Corey, and Francis Nurse are anxious to present their evidence against Abigail and the girls. The court has just condemned Martha Corey and Rebecca Nurse, and, now that

Elizabeth is in jail, Abigail has only to wait until Elizabeth's execution for her plan to be complete. Proctor will finally be free to remarry, and Abigail can possess him. Proctor senses this and is desperate to prove that Abigail is a fraud.

**Character Insight**

Danforth and Hathorne's participation in the court empowers them. The workings of the court concern them more than the actual individuals participating in the proceedings—whether voluntarily or against their will. As a result, when Nurse tells them that the girls have faked the entire witchcraft incident, the judges regard him as a dangerous individual. He casts doubt on the court, its proceedings, and, by extension, Danforth and Hathorne.

## Glossary

**daft** insane; crazy is closer to mad or crazy.

**contentious** always ready to argue; quarrelsome.

**contemptuous** full of contempt; scornful; disdainful. Here, the word describes Giles Corey's attempt to disrupt the court.

**break charity** to treat wrongfully or betray.

# Act III
# Scene 2

## Summary

Proctor and Mary Warren enter the vestry room. Proctor tells Danforth that Mary Warren did not see spirits. Although Danforth refuses to accept Mary Warren's signed deposition, he does agree to talk with her.

Danforth asks Mary Warren about the spirits that she saw. She tells him that she and the other girls only pretended to see spirits. Danforth also questions Proctor to find out if he is trying to undermine the court. He warns Proctor that anything he is hiding will come out. Proctor states that the court is condemning people solely on the basis of children's accusations.

Danforth informs Proctor that Elizabeth claims she is pregnant. Even though the court physically examined Elizabeth, it could not find any sign to prove her pregnancy. Proctor tells Danforth that she "will never lie." Danforth agrees to let Elizabeth live for another year, because of the unborn child.

Proctor gives Danforth a testament stating that Rebecca Nurse and Martha Corey are good, upright women. Ninety-one people have signed the document. Parris argues that the court should summon these people because they question the court. Francis Nurse is upset because he himself promised them that no reprisal would come for from signing the document.

Danforth reads Giles Corey's deposition. Thomas Putnam is brought into the room. Corey accuses Putnam of prompting his daughter to falsely accuse George Jacobs of witchcraft. Corey claims that Putnam wants Jacobs to hang, because anyone hung for witchcraft loses all property rights. Putnam is the only person in Salem who can afford to purchase Jacobs' land once it becomes available. Putnam denies the charge and Danforth requires proof from Corey. Corey refuses to name the individual who overheard Putnam. The court arrests Corey for contempt of court.

Hale tells Danforth that people fear the court. Danforth becomes angry and states that only the guilty should be afraid. Hale disagrees and tells Danforth that not everyone who the girls accuse can be guilty.

Danforth reads Mary Warren's deposition. The deposition states that she never saw the Devil and that the other girls are lying. Hale states that a lawyer should present Proctor's important claim. Hale and Danforth argue over this. After reading the deposition, Parris demands that the court allow him to question Mary Warren. Danforth becomes angry with Parris and denies his request.

Danforth warns Mary Warren that she must tell the truth. He also informs her she will go to jail for committing perjury, whether during her previous testimony or now.

## Commentary

**Character Insight**

Tension arises when Danforth questions Mary Warren and she admits that she and the others have been lying. Danforth believes that he is a fair judge, open to the truth. However, Mary Warren's recant forces him to doubt his own actions. He agrees to listen to Proctor because his claim affects the entire court and its proceedings. His willingness to hear Proctor and render judgment after Proctor has provided his evidence demonstrates that Danforth strives for some amount of fairness. However, the situation troubles Danforth because, if Proctor proves that the accusations have been false, then Danforth must admit that the girls have deceived him. Such an admission would prove him to be a poor judge of character, if children can fool him. Also, the fact that he sent innocent people to the gallows would certainly demonstrate his failure as a judge.

A sharp contrast exists between Parris and Hale. Although not perfect, Hale centers his actions on others. Parris, on the other hand, is self-centered and narrow-minded. He is unbalanced during this scene, and, as the play progresses, he becomes fanatical as he attempts to preserve his position and authority within Salem. During this scene, Parris demonstrates that he still holds a grudge against Proctor. Rather than considering the implications of Proctor's claim that the girls are lying, Parris tries to discredit Proctor. Parris perceives Proctor as the chief member of the faction that opposes him within Salem. Parris will do anything to protect himself and his position as minister.

Theme

Greed and the quest for power also appear again with the exchange between Corey, Putnam, and Danforth. Danforth faces a difficult situation because yet another accuser has been claimed to be acting upon a hidden agenda. Corey has a witness who overheard Putnam talking about obtaining land as a result of his daughter Ruth accusing George Jacobs of witchcraft. This vital information reveals that Ruth is pretending that spirits attack her, and also casts doubt upon the Putnams' claim against Rebecca Nurse. Not only does this suggest that the Putnams fabricated their charge against Rebecca, but it supports the idea that they did it to obtain land. Putnam is opportunistic and willing to profit from the misfortune of others.

Literary Device

Irony emerges when Corey refuses to name his source. Corey's charge against Putnam provides enough information to end the witch trials, if Danforth would analyze the evidence. However, Danforth dismisses the charge against Putnam because of a lack of proof. Ironically, up until this point the court has been condemning people without proof, relying solely on the testimony of children.

## Glossary

**deposition**  the testimony of a witness.

**discontent**  dissatisfaction or restlessness. Here, the verb form is used, meaning to fail to satisfy.

**sharp**  clearly defined; distinct; clear. Here, the word means decisive.

**probity**  uprightness in one's dealings; integrity.

**perjury**  the willful telling of a lie while under lawful oath or affirmation to tell the truth in a matter material to the point of inquiry.

# Act III
# Scene 3

## Summary

Danforth summons Abigail and three of the girls into the vestry room, where he questions Abigail. She denies Mary Warren's charge that she is lying and that she falsely accused Elizabeth Proctor.

Danforth learns that the girls danced in the woods. Hathorne questions Mary Warren and asks her to pretend to faint. When she cannot, he insists that she is lying now because she cannot faint as she claims to have done before.

Danforth asks Abigail if she could have imagined the spirits. Abigail denies such a possibility. Suddenly Abigail and the other girls claim that Mary Warren is sending out her spirit against them.

Proctor calls Abigail a whore and tells the court about their affair. He then defends his wife Elizabeth by saying that she is incapable of lying. The court summons Elizabeth. When she enters the room, no one will speak and she notices that Proctor and Abigail both have their backs to her. When Danforth asks Elizabeth why she dismissed Abigail, Elizabeth lies, concealing Proctor and Abigail's affair.

Abigail and the girls again begin accusing Mary Warren, who recants again and claims that Proctor forced her to say that Abigail is lying. Danforth asks Proctor if he is in league with the Devil, placing Proctor under arrest. Hale denounces the proceedings and quits the court.

## Commentary

**Literary Device**

Scene 3 is the most intense scene in the play because everything is revealed, and timing proves to be one of the most important factors. Proctor realizes that it is critical for Mary Warren to testify against Abigail before she loses her courage to do so. In addition, time is critical at this point in the play because individuals are being convicted continuously. Every conviction increases Abigail's authority and decreases the likelihood that the court will acquit someone accused. Proctor knows that Mary Warren is unsure about testifying directly against Abigail. Just as Danforth appears to favor Abigail's claim that Mary Warren is lying, Proctor informs him that Parris caught Abigail and the others dancing in the woods. This information, coupled with the fact that Parris discovered them, profoundly affects Danforth. Now Danforth views Abigail differently, and is more inclined to believe Proctor.

Danforth's sympathy shifts again to Abigail during Hathorne's cross-examination of Mary Warren. Hathorne makes a legitimate request when he asks Mary Warren to repeat her fainting performance. If she pretended to faint the first time, then she should be able to do it again. She is not able to do it.

Mary Warren's inability to faint or stage a fit serves as a cue to Abigail. In the court's eyes, Mary's failure to feign an attack proves that the girls cannot fake such behavior, which lends merit to Abigail's subsequent claim that Mary Warren's spirit is attacking her. At this point, the court is likely to discard Mary Warren's testimony in view of the evidence Abigail provides.

Only when Proctor accuses Abigail of being a whore does she end her fit and lose credibility with Danforth. When Proctor tells the court of his affair and Abigail's plot to kill Elizabeth, he gives the court another opportunity to end the trials. However, just as Danforth willingly dismissed Corey's claim against Putnam because Corey would not reveal his witness, so Danforth dismisses Proctor's claim that Abigail is a harlot, simply because Elizabeth lies to conceal the affair.

**Literary Device**

Irony is evident in this scene because Danforth is committed to preserving truth, yet he will not acknowledge truth when he hears it. Proctor, who has spent seven months concealing his affair with Abigail, now tells the truth but is disbelieved. And Elizabeth, who has lived by the truth, lies to keep her husband's secret and condemns them both by doing so. And Mary Warren, who had lied and now is finally telling the truth, lies again to save her life. The only winner here is the chief liar, Abigail Williams, who continues to lie. And the court, which should be an instrument of truth, is in the position of condemning those who tell the truth and believing liars.

Truth does triumph in the end, through the individuals who refuse to compromise their beliefs in order to preserve their lives. However, the advocates of truth often pay with their lives—a heavy price.

Proctor's admission of adultery and Elizabeth's lie to hide the affair from the court mark a turning point in their marriage. Shame overwhelms Proctor, but he demonstrates his loyalty and love for Elizabeth by revealing the affair in order to save her life. The situation also changes Elizabeth. She knows that Proctor's name is important to him, and that he would not ruin his reputation by admitting an affair unless he truly loved her. She can finally trust him again.

## Glossary

**guile** slyness and cunning in dealing with others; craftiness; here, deception.

**cool** emotionally uninvolved; uncommitted; dispassionate; here, meaning calculated.

**harlot** a woman who engages in promiscuous sexual activity for pay; here, meaning a sexually immoral woman.

**slovenly** careless in appearance, habits, work, and so on; untidy; slipshod.

**gull** to cheat or trick; dupe.

# Act IV
# Scene 1

## Summary

Act IV begins in the Salem jail. Marshall Herrick wakes up Sarah Good and Tituba to move them to a different cell. Sarah and Tituba tell Herrick that they are waiting for the Devil. They plan to fly to Barbados with the Devil.

## Commentary

Several months have passed since the action in the play began. Act I opened in the spring of 1692, and the season is now fall. The court has already executed twelve people from Salem, and has scheduled seven more to die today.

Although Tituba was told in Act I that she would be spared if she revealed her alliance with the Devil, along with her knowledge of other individuals "in truck" with the Devil, she has in fact been imprisoned. Sarah and Tituba have been in prison so long that they have come to believe that they are in league with the Devil. Cold weather, deplorable living conditions, and the lack of food have made them delusional. They tell Herrick that the Devil will transform them into birds so that they can fly to Barbados. Having internalized the accusations of witchcraft, they now use them to create an escape from their situation.

**Literary Device**

Herrick's willingness to join Sarah and Tituba is noteworthy because he is no longer afraid of the idea of the Devil, nor is he afraid of Sarah or Tituba. At this point in the play the paranoia only remains within the court. The people of Salem have grown weary of the witch trials and the atmosphere of fear and uncertainty they have created.

## Glossary

**rile** to anger; irritate.

## Act IV
# Scene 2

## Summary

Parris summons Danforth and Hathorne and informs them that Hale is attempting to convince the prisoners to confess their crimes. Parris also tells Danforth that Abigail and Mercy Lewis have disappeared. Abigail robbed Parris, and he believes she and Mercy boarded a ship.

Danforth and Parris discuss a recent rebellion in Andover. Parris worries that the people of Salem will throw out the court, as the people in Andover did. He tells Danforth the townspeople are not happy about the upcoming execution of Rebecca Nurse and John Proctor. Parris found a dagger outside his door and he fears for his life. He attempts to convince Danforth to postpone the executions until Hale successfully convinces a prisoner to confess. Danforth refuses.

## Commentary

Theme

Some individuals, such as Putnam, profited from the witch trials, but overall the proceedings have devastated Salem. The court has torn apart families, leaving children as orphans. Fields now stand empty, and cattle roam the streets unclaimed. These consequences are noteworthy because originally the people believed that the trials would only affect the accused; however, one cannot ignore the relationship between the trials and the community. Instead of eliminating evil within the Salem community and uniting the people, the trials created an atmosphere of terror and destroyed the bond between neighbors.

Although no one has attempted to oust the court, as in Andover, grumblings of dissatisfaction echo throughout Salem, and apprehension looms over the court. The people of Salem are tired of living in fear. The court has accused many people, and executed twelve. Proctor has been in jail for three months, giving the people in the town time to think about his charge against Abigail and what happened in Act III, Scene 3. The townspeople no longer believe that Abigail serves as a mouthpiece for God, but instead acts upon her own vengeance; the people have had enough. The dagger that Parris finds represents the potential for violence that is just below the surface in Salem.

Danforth and Parris realize that public sentiment for the court is shifting. Their actions at this point are notable. Danforth displays a rigid determination to continue with the court proceedings. Act III, Scene 1, established the fact that Danforth's own role in the court concerns him more than the implications of the court's actions. Act IV, Scene 2 underscores his earlier behavior. He believes a delay in the executions will suggest he is weak and that he doubts his own judgments. This point should be irrelevant when contrasted with the possibility of executing an innocent person, but public perception of himself concerns Danforth more than justice.

**Character Insight**

Scene 2 continues to contrast Parris and Hale. Self-preservation motivates Parris, while a desire to make things right drives Hale. Parris prevails upon Danforth for a delay, not because he worries about condemning innocent people to die, but because Parris fears for his life. At the beginning of the play Parris worries about a faction trying to force him out of Salem. Now he fears that a mob will attack and kill him. The size of his congregation has diminished. This decrease is due in part to a dissatisfaction with Parris as minister; however, it also underscores the people's dissatisfaction with the court because the people perceive Parris as a proponent of the court.

Abigail's disappearance further testifies to the unrest in Salem. After Proctor revealed their affair, Abigail lost credibility in the eyes of the people, if not the eyes of the court. Abigail now realizes that Proctor thwarted her plan. Not only has she lost all of the power she gained through the witch trials, but she has also lost the prize she sought in the first place, Proctor. Rather than eliminate Elizabeth, her actions have condemned Proctor to hang. The deception that she created to possess Proctor and gain power in Salem has backfired. No reason exists for Abigail to remain in Salem any longer. Hints of violence toward Parris also alert Abigail that the people of Salem may turn against her, because they see her as the one who started the calamity.

Parris does not tell Danforth of Abigail's disappearance immediately because he knows Danforth could interpret it as proof that the girls are a fraud. Once again Parris protects his own interests. He withholds the truth in order to prevent upheaval in Salem—an upheaval he fears would result in violence toward himself. Nevertheless, he has gone from a man who asked for more pay at the start of the play to a man who has lost everything. He is paying for his lack of integrity.

Danforth's reaction to Abigail's disappearance recalls his actions in Act III, Scenes 2 and 3. He does not consider the implications of Abigail leaving Salem because such consideration would force him to review the court and its actions. Carrying on as if he knew nothing of Abigail's disappearance is easier because it allows him to feel secure in his own actions. He will not delay the executions for fear that the people may regard the previous twelve executions as wrong. If this happened, Danforth would lose credibility. He is willing to execute seven more people, even though he doubts their guilt since the flight of their chief accuser.

# Glossary

**strongbox**   a heavily made box or safe for storing valuables.

**gibbet**   a gallows; a structure like a gallows, from which bodies of criminals already executed were hung and exposed to public scorn.

# Act IV
# Scene 3

## Summary

Hale informs Danforth that none of the prisoners will confess. Hale asks Danforth to pardon the seven individuals condemned to die, or allow him more time to persuade them to confess. Danforth refuses.

Hale summons Elizabeth. He asks her to convince Proctor to admit his guilt so that the court will not hang him. Elizabeth agrees to speak with him. Proctor and Elizabeth discuss their children and the child she carries.

Proctor admits that he is considering confessing. He asks Elizabeth if she will respect him if he does. Elizabeth states that it is his decision, and she tells him that she has forgiven him for the affair. Elizabeth realizes that she bears part of the blame for the affair because she has been a cold, suspicious wife in response to her own insecurities.

## Commentary

Scene 3 reveals a dramatic change in the relationship between Proctor and Elizabeth. They have learned to forgive one another and to communicate their feelings. Elizabeth realizes that she cannot blame Proctor entirely for the affair. Her insecurity prevented her from trusting Proctor and her lack of emotion created distance between them. When Elizabeth tells Proctor of her feelings, he sees that Elizabeth no longer condemns him. He can believe her when she tells him she has forgiven him; as a result, they manage to put the affair in the past and move on to consider the future.

Proctor's decision to confess seems surprising at first. Considering his options, however, the choice seems less surprising. The Salem court states that it will find an individual innocent, provided that he or she is of "good conscience," but this is not the case. Danforth tells Hale in Act III, Scene 2 that witchcraft is "an invisible crime," one without witnesses. As a result, once an individual stands accused of witchcraft, he or she is guilty. The Salem court does not operate on the modern idea that an individual is innocent until proven guilty, but that an individual is guilty once accused. As a result, confession is the only way to plea-bargain for one's life.

Proctor is guilty of witchcraft because of his charge against Abigail and Mary Warren's accusation. He can refuse to plead guilty and be hung for witchcraft, or he can confess the crime and live. Either way the court declares him guilty, but the confession shows repentance for the crime and saves him from execution. Both Proctor and Elizabeth realize that lying about the confession is a small price to pay for his life. They have finally reached a point where they can begin to rebuild their marriage, and they do not want to lose that opportunity now.

## Glossary

**floundering** speaking or acting in an awkward, confused manner, with hesitation and frequent mistakes; here, meaning wavering, especially from indecision or doubt.

**quail** to draw back in fear; lose heart or courage; cower.

**disputation** a discussion marked by formal debate, often as an exercise; here, meaning an argument.

# Act IV
# Scene 4

## Summary

Proctor confesses orally to witchcraft, but refuses to implicate any-one else. Danforth informs him that the court needs proof of his confession in the form of a signed, written testimony. Proctor confesses verbally to witchcraft, and Rebecca Nurse hears the confession. She is shocked by Proctor's actions, and she still refuses to confess to witchcraft. Proctor signs his name to the confession, but destroys the document when he learns the court will post it on the church door.

The authorities of the court take Proctor out of the prison toward the gallows. Hale pleads with Elizabeth to convince Proctor to change his mind. Elizabeth refuses. She sees that he is now at peace with himself.

## Commentary

When Proctor tells Elizabeth that he will confess, she understands that he is doing so because he wants them to go home and reestablish their family. Note that neither Proctor nor Elizabeth considers Elizabeth's situation. The court has delayed her execution until she gives birth to the child, but she is still scheduled to hang. If Proctor confesses and gains release, Elizabeth will still remain in jail. Proctor realizes that Elizabeth will not confess, but agrees to confess anyway. The play suggests, but does not confirm, two possible solutions for Elizabeth. First, she may decide that, although lying is a sin, lying to save her life and protect her family justifies the sin—especially since she already lied in the courtroom. On the other hand, perhaps the witch trials will end (as they have in Andover) and the courts will release her. Unfortunately neither one of these happens.

Scene 4 exemplifies a struggle. Proctor knows that signing the confession is lying, and this sacrifice of honor is the hardest for him to bear. His desire to remain honest and his desire to preserve his family tear him in two. Proctor believes that God will forgive him if he confesses, because, as Hale states, "life is God's most precious gift; no principle, however glorious, may justify the taking of it."

Character
Insight

Proctor does not consider himself righteous, in fact he recoils from the idea that he is compared to individuals like Rebecca Nurse who are innocent of any wrongdoing. Of course Proctor has not practiced witchcraft; however, according to himself he is a fallen man, one who has sinned against his wife and himself.

He is willing to sacrifice his honor—which he has already done by admitting to adultery—and he can live with the knowledge that others will view him differently if he confesses. However, Proctor cannot bear the shame of having his confession nailed to the church door. Because confessing will save his life, he can live with that idea, but he believes nailing his confession to the church door constitutes a betrayal of everyone who refuses to confess. A public display of his false confession—especially at a church that is supposed to uphold truth—would insult those who choose to die to preserve their honor. A public display of his signature will strip him of his pride and identity. He will lose his good name and be nothing but a broken man. Proctor's decision to destroy the confession demonstrates his commitment to truth and his inability to tolerate falsehood, especially in himself.

## Glossary

**scaffold** a raised platform on which criminals are executed, as by hanging.

**damn** to cause the ruin of; make fail.

**purge** to cleanse or rid of impurities, foreign matter, or undesireable elements.

**weighty** of great significance or moment; serious.

**beguile** to mislead by cheating or tricking; deceive.

# CHARACTER ANALYSES

# Abigail Williams

Abigail Williams is the vehicle that drives the play. She bears most of the responsibility for the girls meeting with Tituba in the woods, and once Parris discovers them, she attempts to conceal her behavior because it will reveal her affair with Proctor if she confesses to casting a spell on Elizabeth Proctor. Abigail lies to conceal her affair, and to prevent charges of witchcraft. In order to avoid severe punishment for casting spells and adultery—not to mention attempted murder when she plots Elizabeth's death—Abigail shifts the focus away from herself by accusing others of witchcraft. This desperate act of self-preservation soon becomes Abigail's avenue of power.

Abigail is the exact opposite of Elizabeth. Abigail represents the repressed desires—sexual and material—that all of the Puritans possess. The difference is that Abigail does not suppress her desires. She finds herself attracted to Proctor while working in the Proctor home. According to the Puritanical mindset, Abigail's attraction to Proctor constitutes a sin, but one that she could repent of and refuse to acknowledge. Abigail does the opposite. She pursues Proctor and eventually seduces him.

Abigail's willingness to discard Puritan social restrictions sets her apart from the other characters, and also leads to her downfall. Abigail is independent, believing that nothing is impossible or beyond her grasp. These admirable qualities often lead to creativity and a thirst for life; however, Abigail lacks a conscience to keep herself in check. As a result, she sees no folly in her affair with Proctor. In fact, Abigail resents Elizabeth because she prevents Abigail from being with Proctor.

Abigail gives new meaning to the phrase "all is fair in love and war." She has brooded over her sexual encounter with Proctor for seven months. The more she thinks about the affair, the more Abigail convinces herself that Proctor loves her but cannot express his love because of Elizabeth. Abigail continues to review and edit her memories until they accurately portray her as the center of Proctor's existence. Rather than seeing herself as an awkward seventeen year-old who took advantage of a man's loneliness and insecurity during his wife's illness, Abigail sees herself as Proctor's true love and his ideal choice for a wife. She believes she has only to eliminate Elizabeth so that she and Proctor can marry and fulfill her fantasy.

Abigail's fantasy reflects her age. She is a young girl daydreaming about the ideal male. However, she possesses shrewd insight and a capacity for strategy that reveal maturity beyond that of most other characters. Declaring witchcraft provides her with instant status and recognition within Salem, which translates into power. Abigail uses her authority to create an atmosphere of fear and intimidation. She threatens the other girls with violence if they refuse to go along with her plans, and she does not hesitate to accuse them of witchcraft if their loyalty proves untrue. Such is the case with Mary Warren.

Abigail develops a detailed plan to acquire Proctor and will stop at nothing to see her plan succeed. Her strategy includes establishing her credibility with the court and then eliminating Elizabeth. The achievement of her plot requires cold calculation, and so Abigail carefully selects the individuals that she accuses in order to increase her credibility. Thus, she first accuses the town drunk and vagrant, knowing that society is already predisposed to convict them. Each arrest strengthens her position, and demonstrating fits and trances increases her authority even more. Her decision to wait until the court sees her as irrefutable before she accuses Elizabeth reveals her determination and obsession with Proctor. Abigail thinks nothing of the fact that she condemns innocent people to die; those people merely serve as necessary instruments for her use in the fulfillment of her plan. At the end of the play, when Abigail realizes that her plan has failed and that she has condemned Proctor to hang, she displays the same cold indifference that governs her actions throughout the play. She flees Salem, leaving Proctor without so much as a second glance.

# John Proctor

John Proctor is a tormented individual. He believes his affair with Abigail irreparably damaged him in the eyes of God, his wife Elizabeth, and himself. True, Proctor did succumb to sin and commit adultery; however, he lacks the capacity to forgive himself. Unsurprisingly, his relationship with Elizabeth remains strained throughout the majority of the play. He resents Elizabeth because she cannot forgive him and trust him again, but he is guilty of the same thing. In fact, his own inability to forgive himself merely intensifies his reaction to Elizabeth's lack of forgiveness.

In addition to struggling with the weight of his sin, the fact that he must reveal his transgression torments Proctor. His best possession is his good name and the respect and integrity associated with it. Once he acknowledges his affair with Abigail, Proctor effectively brands himself an adulterer and loses his good name. He dreads revealing his sin because guilt and regret already overwhelm him. Proctor believes a public display of his wrongdoing only intensifies the extent of his sin, thereby multiplying his guilt.

Proctor's decision to tell the court about his affair ironically demonstrates his goodness. He willingly sacrifices his good name in order to protect his wife. Only through his public acknowledgment of the affair does Proctor regain his wife's trust. At the end of the play, Proctor refuses to slander himself by allowing the court to nail his false confession to the church door. This action further exemplifies Proctor's integrity. Proctor knows that he will damn himself, yet again, if he agrees to confess. Although he wants to live, escaping death is not worth basing the remainder of his life on a lie. This realization, along with Elizabeth's forgiveness, enables Proctor to forgive himself and finally regain his good name and self-respect. As the court officials lead him to the gallows, he finds peace for the first time in the play.

# Reverend Hale

Reverend Hale's faith and his belief in the individual divide him. Hales comes to Salem in response to a need. He is the "spiritual doctor" summoned to evaluate Salem. His job is to diagnose witchcraft if it is present, and then provide a necessary cure through conversion or by removing the "infected" inhabitants from Salem. Hale devotes himself to his faith and his work. His good intentions and sincere desire to help the afflicted motivate him.

Unfortunately, Hale is also vulnerable. His zeal for discovering witchcraft allows others, particularly Abigail, to manipulate him. The amount of evidence for witchcraft when he arrives in Salem overwhelms him. Although Hale remains determined not to declare witchcraft unless he can prove it, the expectations of the people of Salem sweep him up, and, as a result, he takes their evidence at face value, rather than investigating it himself.

The audience should not condemn Hale. Like Proctor, he falls— through his inaccurate judgments and convictions—but later attempts to correct his shortcomings. Hale is the only member of the court who questions the court's decisions. He is not a rebel, nor does he want to overthrow the court's authority, but he is striving for justice. Once he realizes that Abigail is a fraud, Hale devotes himself to attempting to persuade the other prisoners to confess so that they may avoid execution—using lies to foil lies. What he does not realize is that the lies he is urging would only reinforce the slanders the court has already committed. There would be no truth left.

The action of the play severely tests Hale's faith and understanding. He must acknowledge that children have manipulated his own irrefutable beliefs, while also realizing that he has sent innocent people to their death. This knowledge is a heavy burden, but it changes Hale for the better. Although he questions his own faith and doctrine, he does not abandon religion altogether. He catches a glimpse of true faith through those he has condemned, particularly Rebecca Nurse and Elizabeth Proctor.

# CRITICAL ESSAYS

# Miller's Narrative Technique

Each stage production of *The Crucible* differs from every other in two areas. First, directors stage the play according to their own styles, using various props and costumes while suggesting numerous interpretations of characters. Secondly, individual actors read the lines differently, using diverse voice inflections, gestures, and body language to give each interpretation its own style.

Miller also provides yet another opportunity for variety, not just for the director and actors, but also for the audience and reader. Lengthy exposition pieces that are not glossed as stage directions periodically appear in the written play. For example, at the beginning of Act I, Miller provides stage directions for the set, props, and position of Parris and Betty on stage. However, Miller also includes an extensive psychological profile of Parris prior to beginning the action of the play. Before Parris speaks, a narrator says that "in history he cut a villainous path, and there is very little good to be said for him." Later, the narrator interrupts the action in Scene 1 to include background information on Putnam, and the narrator does the same for Proctor in Scene 3, Rebecca in Scene 4, and Hale and Giles in Scene 5. In addition to historical background on significant characters, the interruptions also include social commentary within the exposition.

The question arises whether or not a director should include these narrative sections, some of which are four pages long, within the play itself. At first glance, it appears that they are to be included within the actual production. If so, then a narrator character must read the narrative sections to the audience. If this is done, however, the continual interruptions in the play's action make engaging the audience in the play difficult. Therefore, the narrative sections should clearly serve only as a tool to provide directors and actors with background information.

The explicative passages allow directors and actors to focus on character motivation, providing them a better understanding of the characters and the historical period. Characters are more engaging because a genuine basis for tension between them exists. For example, obvious tension exists between Thomas Putnam and several other characters in the play, especially Francis Nurse. An actor playing Thomas Putnam must create a persona driven by greed. If the actor knows the passage that states that Putnam was "a deeply embittered man" who attempted to challenge his father's will because his father left the largest portion of money to his stepbrother, then the actor can internalize this quality of Putnam. These background passages result in a more effective portrayal of greed and a more believable character.

Individuals reading the play will have a different experience than the traditional audience because they will read the background information, which will inevitably affect their interpretation of the characters and the play's events. Within the exposition sections Miller addresses the reader directly, in the comfortable, reliable voice of a trusted narrator. As a result, the reader internalizes the information and responds to the characters and their actions based upon it. For example, a reader will discover the same information as a potential actor in regard to Putnam—that Putnam's father left the largest amount of money to Putnam's stepbrother. The reader will also benefit from the narrator's commentary. The narrator tells the reader that the real Putnam accused a large number of people during the trials, often as a method of retaliation or personal gain. After revealing Putnam's historical background, the narrator begins to suggest that Putnam's character will falsely accuse someone within the play. Although the narrator does not finish the suggestion—he only says, "especially when"—the reader automatically expects Putnam to falsely accuse someone in the play. As a result, the reader projects the narrator's commentary onto Putnam's character and anticipates Putnam's false accusations against rival landowners.

## Historical Period: Puritans in Salem

The action of the play takes place in Salem, Massachusetts in 1692. Salem is a Puritan community, and its inhabitants live in an extremely restrictive society. Although the Puritans left England to avoid religious persecution, they established a society in America founded upon religious intolerance. Government and religious authority are virtually inseparable, and individuals who question local authority are accused of questioning divine authority. The Puritan community considers physical labor and strict adherence to religious doctrine the best indicators of faithfulness, honesty, and integrity.

Puritan society stresses the sense of community that results from shared experiences and beliefs. As an unsurprising result, the church dominates the Puritan culture. The church provides individuals with common shared experiences via the Scriptures, and a communal source of morality based on shared values. Thus, a sermon serves as a tool to teach a biblical lesson, and the theocratic government reinforces the precepts from the sermon.

For example, a sermon focusing on the fall of Adam and Eve might discuss the danger of physical gratification and the imminent disobedience resulting from desire. By extension, Puritan society discourages individuality, as well as individual desires. In fact, Puritans consider material and sexual desires unnatural and evil—the Devil's work—and a threat to society. Thus, the society punishes anyone who pursues material and/or sexual gratification. Of course, ways around these rules do exist. As demonstrated in *The Crucible,* people can pursue and obtain what they want without fear of reprisal, so long as they do it under the guise of the church or God's will. However, in general, one can describe Salem as a rigid society, emphasizing work and the suppression of individual desires.

# CliffsNotes Review

Use this CliffsNotes Review to test your understanding of the original text, and reinforce what you've learned in this book. After you work through the review and essay questions, identify the quote section, and the fun and useful practice projects, you're well on your way to understanding a comprehensive and meaningful interpretation of Miller's *The Crucible.*

## Q&A

1. What prompted Proctor to end his affair with Abigail?

2. Why was Goody Putnam jealous of Goody Nurse?

3. Why did Mary Warren accuse Proctor of being the Devil's man?

4. Who was the first person to accuse someone of witchcraft? Who did she accuse?

5. How did Abigail claim that Elizabeth tried to kill her?

   **Answers:** (1) He felt guilty and wanted to become right with Elizabeth and with God. (2) Goody Nurse had eleven children, and all survived. Goody Putnam had eight and lost seven. (3) Abigail was threatening to name her as a witch. (4) Tituba accused Sarah Good. (5) Abigail was struck with a needle in the abdomen that she claimed was caused by Elizabeth sticking a needle in a doll and using witchcraft.

## Identify the Quote

Identify the speaker, listener(s), and the importance of the following quotes in the context of the play.

1. "There is a murdering witch among us, bound to keep herself in the dark."

2. "Spare me! You forget nothin' and forgive nothin'. Learn charity woman."

3. "Is the accuser always holy now? Were they born this morning as clean as God's fingers? I'll tell you what's walking Salem—vengeance is walking Salem. We are what we always were in Salem, but now the little crazy children are jangling the keys of the kingdom, and common vengeance writes the law!"

**4.** " . . . a person is either with this court or he must be counted against it, there be no road between. This is a sharp time, now, a precise time—we live no longer in the dusky afternoon when evil mixed itself with good and befuddled the world."

**Answers:** (1) *Act I, Scene 1.* Putnam is speaking to Parris. Mrs. Putnam and Abigail are also present. This quote is important because it foreshadows the imminent witch trials. Ironically, Putnam refers to one individual woman being responsible for havoc in Salem. Abigail is the metaphorical "murdering witch" because she encourages the girls to falsely accuse others, which results in several hangings of innocent people. She also wants to conceal her affair with Proctor and her scheme to have Elizabeth killed so that she can take her place as Proctor's wife. Also note that Putnam makes this statement because he later becomes one of the chief accusers during the trials, and is therefore responsible for murdering innocent people. (2) *Act II, Scene 1.* Proctor is speaking with Elizabeth. The importance of this quote lies in the fact that "charity" is one of the first social customs to suffer and disappear during the witch trials. Neighbors turn against one another and personal gain and/or self-preservation motivate individuals. Within the Proctor household, charity is akin to forgiveness. Proctor and Elizabeth gain both charity and forgiveness when they admit that they are both responsible for their marital problems. (3) *Act II, Scene 4.* Proctor is speaking to Reverend Hale. Elizabeth is present. This quote is important because Proctor verbalizes the absurdity of both the witch trials and the fact that the unsubstantiated testimony of children is condemning innocent people. As a result of Proctor's statement, Hale begins to question the court's proceedings. (4) *Act III, Scene 2.* Deputy Governor Danforth is speaking to Francis Nurse. Judge Hathorne, Parris, Hale, Proctor, Herrick, Cheever, and Mary Warren are also present. This quote demonstrates the irony of the play. Danforth assures Nurse that the court will acquit anyone who is innocent; however, everyone who has been accused has been condemned. The court is so obsessed with the power it has achieved due to the witch trials, that it blinds itself to truth and justice. Abigail and the other girls deceive and manipulate the court until it becomes an instrument of injustice, rather than an upholder of truth.

## Essay Questions

**1.** A crucible is defined as a severe test. Write an essay discussing the significance of the title. What is "the crucible" within the play and how does it bring about change or reveal an individual's true character?

**2.** As a minister, Reverend Parris is supposed to devote himself to the spiritual welfare of the inhabitants of Salem. Write an essay discussing Parris' concerns and motivations. Is he an effective minister?

**3.** Write an essay discussing Proctor's relationship with Abigail. Why did Proctor have an affair, and what prompted him to end his affair with Abigail?

**4.** Compare and contrast Elizabeth Proctor and Abigail Williams. What are their individual positive character traits? Negative character traits? How do they feel about Proctor?

**5.** Elizabeth despises deception. She is a moral woman, devoted to upholding the truth. Discuss Elizabeth's behavior in the court. What prompts her to lie?

**6.** Write an essay discussing Abigail's plan to get rid of Elizabeth. Is the play a fulfillment of the spell she cast in the woods with Tituba?

**7.** Write an essay discussing the effects of the witch trials on Salem. How do the trials affect the community? Government and authority? The church? Individuals?

**8.** In Act IV, Scene 4, Proctor agrees to falsely confess in order to avoid death. He later changes his mind. Explain why he refuses to confess. What is the "shred of goodness" he discovers?

# Practice Projects

**1.** Stage a debate between Rev. Hale and Rev. Parris regarding the nature of witchcraft and the nature of justice.

**2.** Conduct a jury trial of Abigail Williams. Of what should she be charged? Who would serve as judge, jury, prosecutor, etc?

# CliffsNotes Resource Center

The learning doesn't need to stop here. CliffsNotes Resource Center shows you the best of the best—links to the best information in print and online about the author and/or related works. And don't think that this is all we've prepared for you; we've put all kinds of pertinent information at www.cliffsnotes.com. Look for all the terrific resources at your favorite bookstore or local library and on the Internet. When you're online, make your first stop www.cliffsnotes.com where you'll find more incredibly useful information about Miller's *The Crucible*.

## Books and Articles

This CliffsNotes book, published by Hungry Minds, Inc., provides a meaningful interpretation of Miller's *The Crucible*. If you are looking for information about the author and/or related works, check out these other publications:

> Bigsby, Christopher, ed. *The Cambridge Companion to Arthur Miller*. Cambridge: Cambridge University Press, 1997.
>
> This book provides a chronological overview of Miller's plays and focuses on specific themes within the plays. The article on *The Crucible* examines the roles of conscience and community within the play. The book also addresses McCarthyism and its effect on Miller's writings.

## Internet

Check out these Web resources for more information about Arthur Miller, *The Crucible*, and Shakespeare, Hamlet, and the Salem witch trials:

> "Arthur Miller's *The Crucible:* Fact & Fiction," at www.ogram. org/17thc/crucible.shtml. This web page provides information regarding the historical accuracies and inaccuracies of Miller's play. It also includes a bibliography that lists additional sources of information.
>
> "The Crucible Project," http://204.165.132.2:90/crucible/ main3.htm. This web page provides information regarding the background of the play, witch-hunts, and other historical events. In addition, the site includes numerous essay topics and project ideas, as well as multimedia resources.

"Jen's Crucible Home Page," at http://www.geocities.com/CollegePark/Classroom/3085/crucible.html. This web page provides multiple links for both students and teachers. Links include: audio clips of Joseph McCarthy, film reviews of *The Crucible*, an online study guide to *The Crucible*, information on the Arthur Miller Society, and files on witchcraft and the Puritans that can be downloaded.

"Ogram's 17th Century New England Links: Arthur Miller's The Crucible," at www.ogram.org/17thc/miller.shtml. This web page provides multiple links and includes an easy-to-use directory for navigation. Links include: historical information, interviews with Miller, social issues at work within the play, the Arthur Miller Home Page, teaching guides and study guides for the play, project ideas, web-based bulletin boards, electronic mailing lists, and information about the attempt to ban *The Crucible*.

"The Salem Witchcraft Trials," at http://www.law.umkc.edu/faculty/projects/ftrials/salem/salem.htm. This web page provides multiple links and graphics. Links include: historical documents such as arrest warrants and petitions of the accused, death warrants, biographical information for individuals that the play is based upon, and a comprehensive bibliography of books and periodicals dealing with the play, the historical context of the play, and the individual characters within the play.

# Film

**The Crucible.** Dir. Nicholas Hytner. With Daniel Day Lewis, Winona Ryder, and Joan Allen. Twentieth Century Fox, 1996.

# Send Us Your Favorite Tips

In your quest for knowledge, have you ever experienced that sublime moment when you figure out a trick that saves time or trouble? If you've discovered a useful tip that helped you understand Miller's *The Crucible* more effectively and you'd like to share it, the CliffsNotes staff would love to hear from you. Go to our web site at www.cliffsnotes.com and click the Talk to Us button. If we select your tip, we may publish it as part of CliffsNotes Daily, our exciting, free e-mail newsletter. To find out more or to subscribe to a newsletter, go on to the web.

# Index

# CliffsNotes

@ cliffsnotes.com

## CliffsNotes

### LITERATURE NOTES

Absalom, Absalom!
The Aeneid
Agamemnon
Alice in Wonderland
All the King's Men
All the Pretty Horses
All Quiet on the
Western Front
All's Well &
Merry Wives
American Poets of the
20th Century
American Tragedy
Animal Farm
Anna Karenina
Anthem
Antony and Cleopatra
Aristotle's Ethics
As I Lay Dying
The Assistant
As You Like It
Atlas Shrugged
Autobiography of
Ben Franklin
Autobiography of
Malcolm X
The Awakening
Babbit
Bartleby & Benito
Cereno
The Bean Trees
The Bear
The Bell Jar
Beloved
Beowulf
The Bible
Billy Budd & Typee
Black Boy
Black Like Me
Bleak House
Bless Me, Ultima
The Bluest Eye & Sula
Brave New World
Brothers Karamazov

The Call of the Wild &
White Fang
Candide
The Canterbury Tales
Catch-22
Catcher in the Rye
The Chosen
The Color Purple
Comedy of Errors…
Connecticut Yankee
The Contender
The Count of
Monte Cristo
Crime and Punishment
The Crucible
Cry, the Beloved
Country
Cyrano de Bergerac
Daisy Miller &
Turn…Screw
David Copperfield
Death of a Salesman
The Deerslayer
Diary of Anne Frank
Divine Comedy-I.
Inferno
Divine Comedy-II.
Purgatorio
Divine Comedy-III.
Paradiso
Doctor Faustus
Dr. Jekyll and Mr. Hyde
Don Juan
Don Quixote
Dracula
Electra & Medea
Emerson's Essays
Emily Dickinson Poems
Emma
Ethan Frome
The Faerie Queene
Fahrenheit 451
Far from the Madding
Crowd
A Farewell to Arms
Farewell to Manzanar
Fathers and Sons
Faulkner's Short Stories

Faust Pt. I & Pt. II
The Federalist
Flowers for Algernon
For Whom the Bell Tolls
The Fountainhead
Frankenstein
The French
Lieutenant's Woman
The Giver
Glass Menagerie &
Streetcar
Go Down, Moses
The Good Earth
The Grapes of Wrath
Great Expectations
The Great Gatsby
Greek Classics
Gulliver's Travels
Hamlet
The Handmaid's Tale
Hard Times
Heart of Darkness &
Secret Sharer
Hemingway's
Short Stories
Henry IV Part 1
Henry IV Part 2
Henry V
House Made of Dawn
The House of the
Seven Gables
Huckleberry Finn
I Know Why the
Caged Bird Sings
Ibsen's Plays I
Ibsen's Plays II
The Idiot
Idylls of the King
The Iliad
Incidents in the Life of
a Slave Girl
Inherit the Wind
Invisible Man
Ivanhoe
Jane Eyre
Joseph Andrews
The Joy Luck Club
Jude the Obscure

Julius Caesar
The Jungle
Kafka's Short Stories
Keats & Shelley
The Killer Angels
King Lear
The Kitchen God's Wife
The Last of the
Mohicans
Le Morte d'Arthur
Leaves of Grass
Les Miserables
A Lesson Before Dying
Light in August
The Light in the Forest
Lord Jim
Lord of the Flies
The Lord of the Rings
Lost Horizon
Lysistrata & Other
Comedies
Macbeth
Madame Bovary
Main Street
The Mayor of
Casterbridge
Measure for Measure
The Merchant
of Venice
Middlemarch
A Midsummer Night's
Dream
The Mill on the Floss
Moby-Dick
Moll Flanders
Mrs. Dalloway
Much Ado About
Nothing
My Ántonia
Mythology
Narr. …Frederick
Douglass
Native Son
New Testament
Night
1984
Notes from the
Underground

# CliffsNotes™

@ cliffsnotes.com

## Check Out the All-New CliffsNotes Guides